Hard Words for Desperate Times

Jon surgery 5/1/2020
Jon & Stephanie working at home
Scott last day
Medical
Teachers
  World- pandemic
  Parents
  Abuse victims/families in crisis
• Christin + mike - one car
○ Tara - Rachel
○ World
  ○ Draw closer to God
  ○ Grateful
  • People out of work
  ○ Open our eyes to see
      who
  ○ Kids / Panda
  ○ Nursing homes
  ○ Carolyn Schotler - kidney
                        cancer
                        May 15
  ○ Civility

Wycliffe Studies in Gospel, Church, and Culture

GENERAL EDITOR: THOMAS P. POWER

The series entitled Wycliffe College Studies in Gospel, Church, and Culture is intended to present topical subject matter in an accessible form and seeks to appeal to a broad audience. Typically titles in the series derive from sermons given by the faculty of Wycliffe College, Toronto, in its Founders' Chapel. The current volume on Ezekiel is the eighth in the series.

OTHER TITLES IN THE SERIES

Hard Words for Desperate Times

Going Deep with Ezekiel

EDITED BY
Caleb Gundlach

WIPF *&* STOCK · Eugene, Oregon

HARD WORDS FOR DESPERATE TIMES
Going Deep with Ezekiel

Wipf & Stock
An Imprint of Wipf and Stock Publishers
199 W. 8th Ave., Suite 3
Eugene, OR 97401

www.wipfandstock.com

PAPERBACK ISBN: 978-1-5326-9501-8
HARDCOVER ISBN: 978-1-5326-9502-5
EBOOK ISBN: 978-1-5326-9503-2

Manufactured in the U.S.A.   JANUARY 14, 2020

Contents

Abbreviations

2 Bar.	*2 Baruch (Syrian Apocalypse)*
ESV	English Standard Version
m. Hag.	*Mishnah Hagigah*
m. Meg.	*Mishnah Megillah*
NASB	New American Standard Bible
NIV	New International Version
NJPS	*Tanakh: The Holy Scriptures: The New JPS Translation According to the Traditional Hebrew Text*
NRSV	New Revised Standard Version
REB	Revised English Bible

Introduction

CALEB GUNDLACH

SURELY MANY OF US appreciate the kindness of a note of encouragement. Something goes wrong in our lives and a loving person sends an uplifting message that contains, often enough, a familiar biblical passage such as: "'For I know the plans I have for you,' declares the LORD, 'plans to prosper you and not to harm you, plans to give you hope and a future.'" (Jer 29:11, NIV)

As a rather pessimistic person, I recognize the need for a more positive mindset. I have always appreciated optimistic people who meet my negativity with reminders of the gospel. We know from experience that the Bible is a great place to find encouraging words.

The Book of Ezekiel, however, does not make its way into these sorts of notes. When we turn to this prophetic book, we find hard words, a judgmental attitude, and bizarre imagery. In fact, the difficulties it raises have provoked suspicion regarding its place in the canon throughout the ages. Can you imagine receiving a note with the appended verse: "Behold, I am against you and I will draw my sword from its sheath"? (Ezek 21:3, ESV)

Two options present themselves. We might say that the trauma resulting from the fall of Jerusalem and the Babylonian exile (events which form the background to this prophetic book) explains its harsh tone. Perhaps we can explain away the terrible feeling conveyed by the prophet Ezekiel depicting God standing as an enemy, full of rebuke instead of redemptive mercy. Such a message has already served its purpose in a time far removed from ours. Can we just put this offensive book aside and focus on a more encouraging and relevant one such as Isaiah?

These meditations take a different direction. Instead of comfortably ignoring these hard words, they take up the challenge to read Ezekiel as Christian Scripture. What this means is that they seek to read Ezekiel as an inspired witness to the reality of God and of God's relationship to his people, including Israel and the church. Ezekiel becomes, in these meditations, a place where we as the church may encounter God's word for us.

By reading this prophetic book with Christian eyes, the following contributors direct our gaze to aspects of Ezekiel's vision that can enliven our faith. Are the hard words of Ezekiel hard words for us, or does its place in the canon serve as an antique furniture-piece from a by-gone era? A serious reading of this text as Christian Scripture such as displayed here involves hearing Ezekiel's warnings as relevant for the church today. But it also means understanding more clearly what "judgment" entails, for in Ezekiel, as these meditations make clear, judgement is about separation, a life lost in idolatry and a chosen path where God is no longer a living reality. That is to say, judgement is about *losing* something—or someone—the departure of God's glory from the temple and exile from home.

Engaging Ezekiel in this way, however, does not leave us in the terrain of threat and judgment. Rather these meditations show us that the hard words Ezekiel speaks can also lead us to the gospel. In the Book of Ezekiel on the other side of judgement is hope, grounded in the realization that God choses to enter into our dark places. This was certainly the case for the exiles who, in the midst of their tragic circumstances, encountered God addressing them, promising new life, and calling them to conversion. This is the case laid out for us in Ezekiel. God remains present. Despite everything, we are never abandoned.

So it must be said that Ezekiel offers neither optimism nor pessimism but rather reveals a pattern of hope that we too can take hold of as twenty-first century Christians. Wherever we happen to be, conversion and new life are open to us because, to sum up the message of Ezekiel with its own final breath, "Yahweh is there." (Ezek 48:35)

The book of Ezekiel opens with a vision of heaven. In chapter 1 God is seen, appearing (what is more) in human form. Joseph Mangina points us to the extent such a vision would have challenged Israel's theological categories. The vision is bewildering to us as well, "exploding the containers" in which we try to place God. With this vision as its introduction, Mangina discerns that the book establishes a context for reading the prophet's harsh words. In a time of extraordinary trial, Israel, and we too, are reminded of God's glory and his immanent, even corporeal presence.

Turning to the character of Ezekiel himself, Stephen Andrews asks how the prophet's response to God's call can inform our respective callings to serve in the church. Moreover, he asks whether a prophetic office exists for the church today. If so, what does it look like?

From Ezekiel 2–3, he discerns some characteristics of vocation. Like Ezekiel, God's call upon our lives is mediated through our encounter with the word of God, but also through experiences that at times lead us to question our abilities. As in the case of the prophet Ezekiel, such experiences lead us to recognize our "native unsuitability" to our vocational tasks, prompting us to authentic humility. Andrews finds that Ezekiel's prophetic office is not simply a matter of speaking while standing aloof from the people. In addition to declaring the word of God, Ezekiel is "compelled to live according to it." And so for the church, our prophetic role consists not only of "declaration" but of a "demonstration of God's word to the world."

While Stephen Andrews helps us to identify with the prophet, Ephraim Radner's meditation prompts us to identify with those the prophet rebukes. He cautions us that it is not possible to read Ezekiel as *Christian* Scripture and hear the voice of judgment on Israel as some distant past event for an audience other than ourselves. As the Israel in Christ, the Christian church, we must hear these difficult words as part of our own story. Moreover, for those of us who tend to identify with the prophet, reforming and rooting out injustices in the community, we see in the prophet Ezekiel a figure of the cross. God's prophet does not escape the exile. Radner points out that oftentimes we, too, are called to suffer with our communities, shaken and enduring sin's consequences. Ezekiel not only announces judgment but "carries . . . the burden of the judgment he announces in his own body."

Ezekiel does this by dramatic sign-acts wherein he uses his own body to enact God's judgment before a bewildered audience. Marion Taylor considers three of these dramatic sign-acts performed by the prophet in chapter

4 of Ezekiel. To a people already exhausted, Ezekiel announces through these ancient forms of "street theatre" that "they weren't getting home soon." The scene turns into an overwhelming situation of judgement upon judgement as Ezekiel announces a second siege of Jerusalem and a second wave of exiles to Babylon.

How can we as modern Christians find our bearings in all this? Isn't God supposed to be merciful? Marion Taylor shows us that even here, within a difficult passage and difficult circumstances, God reveals himself as one who alleviates burdens. This is on account of God's character, a character that is one and the same, whether in Ezekiel or in the New Testament. No matter our times or circumstances, we have, in heaven, a God who is able to sympathize with our weakness. (cf. Heb 4:15)

Glen Taylor gets specific about what actually went wrong in Israel before the judgment of exile. His meditation focuses on Ezekiel chapter 8 and its depiction of idolatry in the temple. As he shows us, this is idolatry-gone-wild reaching the heights of obscenity and depravity and involving even those in leadership positions!

The story of Israel prompts many questions for us, and Glen Taylor encourages us to take a healthy self-assessment of our own idolatrous tendencies. As communities of faith, do we rationalize our tendency to accommodate the gospel within a relativistic culture? As individuals, do we live as though God does not see? Are we practical atheists who play a game in which we "go through the motions" of church-going and church-speak, but without faith, much as Israel before the exile?

Such a text urges us to get real with God by realizing that God is real. And this need to recognize the reality of God points to what is most at stake in Israel's and our own idolatry. The greatest threat is not the exile and the loss of land, but rather distance from God. As Peter Robinson shows us in his meditation on Ezekiel 9–10, the tragic consequence of idolatry is the loss of glory, that is, the departure of God's glory from the temple in Jerusalem.

How applicable is this to us, he asks, who so easily lose our sense of God's active presence in this world, acting, thinking, and feeling as though God simply is not there even while maintaining the skeleton of faith? Robinson shows us that these words in Ezekiel train us to long for a greater awareness and attentiveness to God's active presence in the world. Such a reality became clear to Ezekiel as God's glory *reentered* the prophet's life, far away from Jerusalem, on the banks of the Chebar River. And such a reality belongs to us, as well, who draw near to Jesus Christ and see in him the active presence of God's glory revealed.

Undoubtedly, anyone familiar with Ezekiel has struggled with some of the images the prophet uses to depict God. The prophet, it could be charged, is misogynistic, not only using the well-worn metaphor of prostitution to describe Israel's unfaithfulness, but depicting God as a vengeful, abusive husband. Kira Moolman walks us through this difficult terrain, focusing on Ezekiel 16. Without excusing this offensive language, she discerns what purpose such a difficult text might serve; it shocks its ancient audience, and us, to full attention, depicting a tragic situation that is the full reversal of the promised covenant: estrangement, suffering, and loss of children in place of closeness to God, the blessing of children, and flourishing in the land.

The theme of conversion, as this is expressed in Ezekiel 18, is taken up by Andrew Witt. In contrast to our apathy towards the living God, Ezekiel tells us to "consider, turn, and live." Such a conversion, Witt shows us, involves "a gloriously free and unqualified call to repentance and a new beginning." In other words, as stark and heavy as Ezekiel's picture of our lives without God can become, nothing, Witt argues, can stand in the way of a path to freedom from our past mistakes. For those of us with a past, Ezekiel 18 is one of the most encouraging texts in the Old Testament. But the path outlined in this text involves repentance and conversion, which is nothing short of turning from death to life.

In Ezekiel 20, the prophet takes on the role of a social gadfly, challenging the traditional founding narratives of Israel. Many have asked why Ezekiel retells Israel's history in this chapter, revised to include a darker depiction of Israel's past. David Kupp concludes that the stories of Israel's triumphant past in the Pentateuch led to a misinterpretation. The common view in Ezekiel's day was that Israel's election in the past meant that losing the land and the Jerusalem temple were simply not possible. In our own day, Kupp argues, the stories we tell ourselves and sustain within our communities tend to include blinders that prevent us from seeing our moral standing in relationship to others clearly. Ezekiel reminds us to listen closely to the word of God lest we simply carry on with these false assumptions and inflated self-perceptions.

The relevance of Ezekiel for leadership in the church today is the theme of Judy Paulsen's meditation on Ezekiel 34. Fulfilling our call to leadership in the church means taking our notes from the Good Shepherd. As Paulsen writes, "He is the one to study." The servant-leader we see in Jesus, Paulsen shows us, is the counter-image of Israel's shepherds rebuked in Ezekiel 34. We find that this text prompts us in the opposite direction, leading us to become servant-leaders who offer up ourselves for others instead of using others for our own desires and self-aggrandizement.

Both Annette Brownlee and Thomas Power move us into the visionary climax of Ezekiel's prophecy, depicting the resurrection of the dry bones and the restoration of the temple. Here we encounter a full-scale reversal of what we saw in the beginning. In place of a complete end through comprehensive judgement, we receive a word of hope through visions that recount a new future, a new creation, and a renewed people.

Considering Ezekiel 37, Annette Brownlee takes us through Ezekiel's vision of resurrection amid mass-graves in the desert. With this text, she underscores the Christian conviction that God's work in history entails a singular pattern, whether in the history of Israel, the history of the church, or the story of our own lives. Certain features of God's redemptive work that are perceived in Ezekiel's text remain the same today, such as God's total initiative in raising us up to new life and the working of God's Spirit in our knowledge and relationship with him.

This brings us finally to Ezekiel 40–48 and Ezekiel's vision of the restored temple, where God returns in glory to remain with his people. As Thomas Power shows us, this is not a simple restoration of what came before. This is especially clear in Ezekiel 47. Out of this new temple flows a torrent of water, immeasurable and bringing healing to everything it touches. Such is a sign of the immeasurable grace available in the New Covenant. These waters run deep and foreshadow the "river of living water" given to us through the Spirit in the New Testament (cf. John 7:38).

Harsh words of judgment, strange images and depictions of God that defy categorization, insight into the ways of trust that mark the community of faith and its hope-filled posture—such features in the book of Ezekiel are drawn out in the following contributions. These meditations help us to see that even in the difficult parts of Scripture, we encounter the same God present to us in Jesus Christ. Even in Ezekiel, we encounter the living God whose work is always to raise up his people to new life.

1

Gazing on the God Who Cannot Be Seen

Ezekiel's Vision by the River Chebar

Joseph Mangina

In the thirtieth year, in the fourth month, on the fifth day of
the month, as I was among the exiles by the river Chebar, the
heavens were opened, and I saw visions of God

—EZEK 1:1

"I" IN THIS CASE meaning of course the prophet Ezekiel,
whose mission to Israel began in the year 593 BCE—after
the first deportation of exiles to Babylon in 598, but before
the final cataclysm of the sacking of Jerusalem and the
destruction of the temple in 587/86. Before you know anything else about Ezekiel, know that he flourished—if that

is the right word—in an age of mayhem and destruction and political as well as religious uncertainty. The world was falling apart, the center did not hold—and what else was Jerusalem but the very center and navel of the cosmos? In short it was your typical prophetic situation, when the question as to whether the LORD stills speaks—or if he does speak, whether anyone will listen—can be evaded no longer.

Ezekiel was a priest, a literate man, and so his is an intricately structured and powerfully written book. It is also, frankly, rather weird in places. The prophet eats food cooked over animal dung (after talking God down from human dung), lies on his side for months at a time, and shaves his hair so that he may burn it, slash it with a sword, and cast it into the wind. He uses his own body as site for a kind of performance art. Ezekiel's language and imagery frequently shock us—and are meant to do so. The reason we bother to struggle with these hard passages is the Christian conviction that Scripture is the LORD's Word to his people, in the twenty-first century no less than in Babylon by the banks of the river Chebar.

The phrase "the Word of the LORD" occurs early on in our reading —"Now the Word of the LORD came to the priest Ezekiel son of Buzi, in the land of the Chaldeans by the river Chebar; and the hand of the LORD was on him there" (1:3). That sounds like your typical "call" formula for an Old Testament prophet. But before that, in verse 1, we are told that the heavens opened and that Ezekiel saw *visions* of God. There is visionary experience in almost all the prophets. The visions are an important corrective to our tendency to suppose that the Word of God is "wordy," that is, chiefly concerned with ideas or principles or doctrines—who knows, perhaps even a kind of critical theory of religion. Well, prophets *do* have the task of sharing God's living word with his people. But the Word of God is not mainly ideas or doctrines. The Word of God is the display of God's being and will for us, in language, yes, but also in visual and even tactile form. The visions of the prophets testify to the overwhelming *reality* of God, who is so real that we cannot stop ourselves from gazing upon him.

But Houston, or rather Babylon, we have a problem here, because isn't the LORD God of Israel supposed to be invisible? There was famously no image of the LORD in the temple, no statue or idol by which he might be identified. Rather, there was the ark of the covenant, and above it the mighty cherubim, and above the cherubim . . . an empty space. That empty space is a rather frightening thing, when you think about it: the sign of a radically transcendent deity, a God who refuses to be boxed in or domesticated. Whatever else the temple or the church may be, neither is a *container* for God. As a priest Ezekiel would have known all about that absent space between the cherubim. But as soon as we note the invisibility of Israel's God we immediately begin to think of all sorts of exceptions to that rule—the theophanies, whether the mysterious visitors to Abraham at Mamre (often taken as an icon of the Trinity), or the LORD revealing his Name to Moses at the Burning Bush, or the LORD on Sinai passing before Moses (who sees, to be sure, only God's "hind parts"), or Isaiah's great vision when he "saw the LORD sitting upon a throne, high and lofty, and the hem of his robe filled the temple" (Isa 6:1).

Within Scripture, it is Isaiah's vision that forms the closest connection to the vision described in Ezekiel 1. There is a big difference, of course. Isaiah has his vision *in* the temple, the "right" place for such an experience to happen, whereas Ezekiel is hundreds of miles away in Babylon. The LORD is not bound by creaturely space and time. But just as God is not simply "invisible," so he is not simply "omnipresent," spread out across the universe like cream cheese on a bagel or a misty fog on a London night. As Robert Jenson notes in his excellent commentary on Ezekiel, God's omnipresence means that the entire creation is but a single place for him.[1] His dwelling is in heaven, but at any moment the distance between heaven and earth may collapse to reveal the LORD's terrifying intimacy with his creatures. The creature's space is drawn into the LORD's space. This is what happens to Ezekiel. He has visions of God.

And what does he see? He sees a throne—*the* throne. The vision unfolds gradually, showing Ezekiel's flair for the dramatic. First he sees a thunderstorm with flashing lightning, reminiscent of the theophany on Sinai. Then, in the midst of the storm, he sees four creatures—these are the cherubim, no longer the gold statues in the temple, but living beings in human form, each with four faces: human, lion, ox, and eagle. (We will meet these creatures again, slightly modified, in the book of Revelation. In later Christian tradition, they will become emblems of the four evangelists.) The creatures have four wings, supporting the dome or firmament above them. But first Ezekiel describes the wheels that accompany each of the creatures, like no wheels on earth, with a wheel within each wheel—whatever that means. Somewhat disconcertingly, the wheels are equipped with eyes all around their rims. I am sure that if you went online you would find quite literal depictions of all this, but don't do it—look it up online, that is—because such literal representation is beside the point. Ezekiel is not

1. Jenson, *Ezekiel*, 33.

drawing a diagram. He is seeking to display the power and majesty of God in the form of word-pictures. The wheels speak of the LORD's transcendence over space and time, his "hypermobility," while the eyes speak of his all-seeing wisdom; the LORD knows things from their insides. Call this omnipresence and omniscience, if you will, although these terms pale in comparison with the vision itself.

The beating wings of the cherubim support a dome, and above the dome we find the throne itself, which however doesn't get much description. Ezekiel simply says that it's "like a sapphire." And on the throne is seated "something that seemed like a human form, like amber from the waist upward, fiery from the waist downward, and surrounded by fire" (1:26-27). The whole scene is alive with color: "Like the bow of a cloud on a rainy day, such was the appearance of the splendor all around" (1:28). In this same verse, the prophet sums up the whole vision saying, "This was the appearance of the likeness of the glory of the LORD."

Who is it that is seated upon the throne? It is, of course, the LORD God of Israel. But why in human form? At this point, we have a fundamental hermeneutical decision to make. We could say that just as all language about God is metaphorical and analogical, a point made commonly enough in theology, so the prophet has no choice but to represent the LORD as a human. God is "like" a human king, only he's not. God rides on a chariot outfitted with angelic wheels and eyes, only of course he doesn't. Ezekiel, in other words, is an early proponent of what we would call metaphorical theology. We speak about God in human terms, which are the only terms available to us, but then constantly remind ourselves of the inadequacy of our images. God himself remains forever hidden behind the images; students who have taken my Systematic Theology class know to call this modalism. God remains distant, unknowable, beyond thought—leaving us with only our religious language and practices. That would be the standard teaching of late modern theology, which is sadly the operative theology of our congregations. All in all it is pretty tame stuff.

But there is a more daring reading of the passage, and you've probably guessed that it's the one I would favor. The Church Fathers, you see, had no doubt as to who sat upon the throne that Ezekiel glimpsed. It was of course Jesus. Not Jesus *instead* of God the Father, but Jesus *as* the Father's perfect image, the Lamb slaughtered and yet victorious, the one who in the book of Revelation is seen to be *sharing* God's throne. It is Christ who is enthroned upon the cherubim with their many eyes, Christ who is the incarnation of the divine power and wisdom and yes, love. But in Ezekiel, perhaps the divine attribute we need most to stress is the sheer weight and substance of the LORD's glory, his *kabod*. "This was the appearance of the likeness of the glory of the LORD." It is an emphasis shared by the Fourth Gospel: "We have beheld his [that is, Christ's] glory, glory as of the only Son from the Father" (John 1:14).

Why are Ezekiel's visions so rich, his descriptions of the being and actions of God so lavish and over the top? Because the incarnation gives him something to describe. In the midst of exile, by the banks of the river Chebar, the LORD who wills to be with and for his people in Jesus Christ is already present. Israel knew the incarnate one, even though he was "not yet" incarnate. If that offends our sense of chronology then so be it, for the Lord has a way of exploding the containers we put him in.

And that is why reading the prophets—even a difficult prophet like Ezekiel—is always an encounter with good news. There is of course lots of bad news in the prophets: sin, rebellion, death and destruction. Ezekiel opens with Israel in Babylon, exiled for their sins. This does not seem a very promising beginning. But into the midst of Babylon, by the banks of the river Chebar, the LORD's chariot appears in a flame of fire. The LORD is with us, and so all is not lost. May we, who also live in Babylon, know his glory and his judgment and his grace, and take comfort in the good news of his coming.

Scripture: Ezekiel 1

Questions for Further Reflection:

1. Can God be seen, or not? Why does the Bible seem to give ambiguous or even conflicting answers to this question?

2. The author of this meditation agrees with the Church Fathers in identifying the human form in Ezekiel's vision with Jesus, who lived centuries later. Is this way of reading the Old Testament legitimate? If it is, how might it challenge some of our commonsense perceptions of time and history?

3. The early Christian heresy called modalism claimed that the persons of the Trinity are only so many "masks" God puts on, not God as God really is. How does the author of the meditation link modalism with metaphor?

4. Read chapters 4 and 5 of the Book of Revelation. What links do you see with Ezekiel? How are the visions different?

2

No Room for Vanity

Ezekiel and the Prophetic Vocation

STEPHEN ANDREWS

You are to say to them, "These are the words of the Lord God," and they will know that they have a prophet among them, whether they listen or whether in their rebelliousness they refuse to listen

—EZEK 2:4–5, REB

IN LIGHT OF THE vision recorded in Ezekiel chapter 1, it is not certain that what we have among us is a lunatic and not a prophet. The description of the prophet's vision resembles more of a fireworks display or a drug trip, or perhaps a fireworks display while taking drugs. Storm winds, brilliant lights, fire, fantastic creatures, fused beast-humans, whirring wheels, bejeweled wheels, wheels within wheels, wheels with eyes, rising, moving, stopping. And the noise. Mighty torrents and thunder claps, the din of an army encampment and the rising of voices. It is understandable why the chapter was banned from being read in the synagogue and from being studied in the schools.[1] One can occasionally wonder whether the church should exercise a similar restriction regarding parts of the book of Revelation.

And yet we are in the presence of a prophet, and the assurance that this is the case is to be found in our passage. For whereas chapter 1 consisted largely of a description of the author's ecstatic vision, in chapter 2 this vision is complemented by a divine word. In chapter 1 we might have concluded that Ezekiel was clearly among the ranks of the mystics, and we may even have wondered, as some scholars do, whether he was suffering from a pathological condition.[2] But now it becomes evident that, as jarring and incoherent as his visions may be, he has been enlisted as a "prophet," for now the word of the Lord addresses him, and God's Spirit fills him, raises him up (2:1–2), and sends him out (3:22).

In the course of meditating on the book of Ezekiel, we are offered many opportunities to deepen our understanding of the nature of biblical prophecy and the calling of the prophet. And we may well ask whether the office of the prophet still exists today, or to what degree Christians may describe their roles in the church and in the world as "prophetic." These important questions will not find

1. *m. Meg.* 4:10; *m. Hag.* 2:1.

2. E.g., David J. Halperin, who suggests Ezekiel was disturbed by sexual longings and fears in *Seeking Ezekiel: Text and Psychology*. For the case that Ezekiel was a paranoid schizophrenic, see Edwin C. Broome, "Ezekiel's Abnormal Personality," 277–292.

satisfactory answers in this morning's passage, and yet there are features of the divine call on Ezekiel's life that may be relevant to anyone seeking the will of God. And many of these features can be found in the testimonies of other biblical figures.

So at the outset, let us say that this twofold manner of communication is characteristic of divine revelation. For it is rare that God's commission comes in words alone or experiences alone. Both are agents of vocation. The words are necessary to interpret the experiences, while the experiences serve the purpose of demonstrating the words. In a phrase perhaps reminiscent of this passage, St. Paul recounts how his journey to Damascus was interrupted by the experience of a blinding light that caused his travelling companions to fall to the ground. This would have been little more than a terrifying vision, except that it was accompanied by a voice from heaven saying, "I am Jesus, whom you are persecuting. But get to your feet, for I have appeared to you for a purpose" (Acts 26:16).[3] The call of God on one's life will inevitably be mediated by both words and experiences, and the conviction that God has issued a summons to us will often be a measure of how these words and experiences illumine each other.

But life is full of both words and experiences. And it is not always possible to make sense of them, or to see how they relate to one another. How is one to know that the call comes from God? That an event is not random? That the explanation of the call is reliable? While there is no infallible litmus test, the story of Ezekiel's commission gives us some helpful ways of thinking about this question. We want to say something, first, about the nature of

3. Cf. 2 Bar. 13:2–3.

vocation in general, and then to touch on the matter of the prophetic vocation.

The first thing to note is that when the word of God comes to Ezekiel at the end of chapter 1, Ezekiel is flat on his face, awed by the divine majesty revealed to him in his vision. It is a posture of abject humility, and embodies a sense of unworthiness at being in the proximity of the divine. The Lord furthermore addresses Ezekiel, particularly in his mortality. "Son of man," he calls him (Ezek 2:1). This is not the messianic title of Daniel or the Gospels, but is used eighty-seven times in the book to underline Ezekiel's creatureliness. It is a reminder that the prophet is the mouthpiece, and nothing more, of the divine will. And in the message of judgement and deliverance that he will be called to convey, his status as a lowly mortal will prevent him thinking that he has any responsibility in implementing the prophecies. For he will be reminded continually that, though his words bear power, they are not his words, it is not his power. Twice in these early verses, God says to Ezekiel, "*I* am sending you" (vv. 3-4). The initiative, words, and power lie with God.

A pitfall in any attempt to discern our vocation is to believe that we somehow merit God's call. A character in one of C.S. Lewis's novels, while reflecting on why he might have been chosen for a particular mission, states that "One never can see, or not till long afterwards, why *any* one was selected for *any* job. And when one does, it is usually some reason that leaves no room for vanity."[4] A former parishioner of mine was designated a Poet Laureate in Saskatchewan, and when I asked him once how he came up with his poetic ideas, he replied that he tried to be the kind of person to whom poetic ideas came.

4. Lewis, *Perelandra*, 22.

Modesty, submissiveness, the awareness of our weaknesses and shortcomings, a fundamental belief in our native unsuitability, these are demeanors conducive to detecting the call of God in our lives.

But this leads us to the question of purpose. "I am sending you," the Lord God said to Ezekiel. But what was God sending Ezekiel to? What was his mission? The answer is, rather simply, that he is given the task of proclaiming God's message. "This generation to which I am sending you is stubborn and obstinate. You are to say to them, 'These are the words of the Lord God'" (v. 4).

Now, we don't know yet what these words entail. Indeed, it is rather remarkable that throughout this chapter and the next, while the commission to "go" is repeated, we are never told what these "words of the Lord God" actually are. In fact, in a grand anticlimax, at the end of chapter 3, when he is bidden to rendezvous with the glory of the Lord in the valley so that the Lord might address him, Ezekiel receives the instruction to go home, lock the doors, and be bound and gagged, so that he shall *not* be able to convey the words of God. Is there such a vocation? A vocation to silence? A calling for inaction?

This too is part of the prophetic commission. For while Ezekiel is not addressing the people of Israel directly with the divine word, he has himself received such a word and is compelled to live according to it. Indeed, God gives him an appetite for this word which, in the dramatic example of the eating of the scroll, is received as a sweet honey sandwich. And in the end, this is a picture of the very essence of biblical prophecy. Prophecy is not just a telling of the future in poetic speech, or a prognostication with a "this is the word of the Lord" slapped on. Prophecy is both the declaration and demonstration of God's word in the world. In his discussion of the prophetic consciousness, Walter Brueggemann calls these "imagination" and "implementation," and they are both components of any truly prophetic commission.[5] For prophecy confronts the world in both the prophet's words and works. One might say that it also conforms to the divine alchemy that brings word and experience together into a single mode of address.

And this may serve as our second insight from the text. For if the first thing we learn is that humility is the substrate of the divine call, the second is that the call, if it is faithfully received, involves both proclamation and obedience. In this respect, every attempt of the Christian to embrace and teach the word of God is an act of prophecy. In this respect, when the church itself seeks to live under and to live out the word of God, it is living prophetically. Even as we sit under judgement or hold on to hope, we are living prophetically, for we are embodying a word of God that points to a Reality that is greater than our own.

Now, as we see many times over in the book of Ezekiel, the prophet's faithful response occasionally, maybe even often, defies human logic and risks offending human pride. We are given some insight into how this works as Ezekiel's story unfolds. While there may be some who heed the prophet's words, God warns Ezekiel that many will refuse to listen; they shall be "brazen and stubborn," (v. 4) for they are a rebellious people. And yet he is not to be discouraged. For the test of a prophecy's legitimacy is not its effectiveness in changing the world. That is God's domain. The prophet's sole responsibility is to discharge his or her duty faithfully. Indeed, God warns Ezekiel that neglect of his prophetic duties will make him responsible for the fate of those who did not receive the divine warning

5. Brueggemann, *The Prophetic Imagination*, 40.

he was sent to deliver. But Ezekiel has every reason to be confident. For, as he was told, it is God's word and not his own that he is bidden to declare. And what is more, God has given him a hard headedness to match their own. His very name, Ezekiel, means "God strengthens." God will give us what we need to be faithful in our seemingly impossible tasks.

So what is the nature of our own vocations? Some of us may struggle with questions of where God is calling us to serve, and in what capacity. Let us be mindful of two important things. The first is that vision will be granted to those who ask in humility, and to those who recognize their own poverty in asking. The second is that vocation involves both words and deeds, both proclamation and obedience. This is not a pastoral or episcopal vocation particularly. It is, rather, the vocation of every Christian who seeks to live by the words of Scripture. It is the vocation of the church herself.

Where is the prophetic Christian in our day? Where is the prophetic church in our community, in our country? There are indeed powerful prophets among us. And I conclude with the example of a Boston pastor who has been in the news recently, on account of his efforts to bring peace and security into the troubled inner city. Eugene Rivers grew up in the Philadelphia slums and was a gang member at the age of twelve. But at the age of thirteen, his life turned a corner when he heard Billy Graham on the radio. A bright lad, Rivers audited classes at Yale and eventually spent three years at Harvard. There, he married Jackie, a Harvard graduate.

In 1984, Eugene and Jackie moved to Dorchester in Boston. It is a notoriously violent neighborhood. There he established the Azusa Christian Community, a "community committed to preaching and teaching the gospel to people of African descent." But life was not easy. The first time the Rivers's home was struck with gunfire that almost hit (their son) Malcolm, a reporter asked Jackie, "What are you going to do?" Eugene looked at her and said, "It's your call." She said, "I feel called by God to be in this neighborhood, and because I feel called, I feel protected. If I'm not where the Lord is calling me, I'm not safe."

In other words, where the Lord calls, the Lord abides. "We recognize," Rivers continued, "that a community of faith that is willing to really follow the leading of the Holy Spirit can make a difference in the worst neighborhood. Dramatic changes will always require dramatic sacrifices. Dramatic blessings have dramatic costs."[6]

In our own longing for God and in the search for our own vocations, God grant us both the humility and courage to go where he leads, for the greater glory of his Son.

Scripture: Ezekiel 2–3

Questions for Further Reflection:

1. Describe the ways your own calling as a follower of Jesus Christ has come through word and experience. Have word and experience been at odds with one another? Have they confirmed one another? In what does your confidence of God's calling rest?

2. In what ways does my pride prevent me from discerning God's call in my life?

3. What is the place of proclamation and obedience in my life? How can these be understood as "prophetic"?

6. Zoba, "Separate and Equal," 23.

3

Hard Words for Desperate Times

MARION TAYLOR

THE OPENING CHAPTERS OF the book of Ezekiel present us with a dramatic account of the prophetic call and commission of a man who had been exiled to Babylon in 598 BC along with the king, his royal entourage, and a number of Judah's important families and citizens. What follows this introduction is an account of Ezekiel's message of doom and judgement. This message takes many forms and continues nonstop until chapter 25 when the prophecies against the foreign nations begin. The message Ezekiel both proclaims and enacts is quite simple: the land of Judah and the city of Jerusalem are going to be attacked a second time by the Babylonians. And those remaining in Judah are going to suffer more destruction and devastation than they had experienced in 598 BC.

Ezekiel's message is very harsh, but it's also curious because it is given to Jews who had already experienced God's judgement and were now living in exile. Most of them were likely suffering from post-traumatic stress disorder. The lives of God's exiled people had been shattered. They were asking questions about why they were in exile, how long the exile would go on, and where God was in their messy lives. They were likely jealous of those left behind in Jerusalem and they were unquestionably anxious to return. They had likely been living in exile for about five years when they witnessed Ezekiel's very strange acts of street theatre that we read about in Ezekiel chapter 4. God's message to them through Ezekiel was not one they wanted to hear as they weren't expecting another Babylonian invasion of Judah, a second siege of Jerusalem, and the total destruction of their beloved temple and city. The author of Psalm 137 expressed their feelings well:

> By the rivers of Babylon we sat and wept
> > when we remembered Zion.
> 2 There on the poplars
> > we hung our harps . . .
>
> 8 Daughter Babylon, doomed to destruction,
> > happy is the one who repays you
> > according to what you have done to us.
> 9 Happy is the one who seizes your infants
> > and dashes them against the rocks.

Ezekiel's audience would not have been pleased to hear his message of doom and judgement because it meant that God's judgement on his people in Judah was not over. It also meant that they would not be returning home soon.

Like many other Old Testament prophets, Ezekiel used a number of different ways to communicate God's message. More than any other Old Testament prophet, Ezekiel used sign actions or sign acts or what we might call today street theatre to communicate God's shocking message that Jerusalem was about to come under siege again and that those living in Judah would experience hunger and eventually be sent into exile where they would live among an unclean people. Ezekiel was a very effective communicator; he was as Ronald Clements suggests very attentive to "the visual side of proclaiming truth. The people must see in order to believe."[1]

Ezekiel chapter 4 contains three dramatic sign actions. In the first one (vv. 1–3), God asks Ezekiel to set up a kind of war-game model. He was to take a block of moist, unbaked clay and draw a map of Jerusalem on it using either a stick or his finger. Then he was to build a siege wall, a ramp, battering rams, and enemy camps around the model of the city. But the war-game model was not yet complete as Ezekiel was to separate himself from the city under siege by placing a heavy iron pan or cooking griddle between himself and his model.

Anyone looking at Ezekiel's model would know its message; they had all lived through Nebuchadnezzar's siege of Jerusalem—they knew Nebuchadnezzar's tactics had worked well as a way to weaken their resistance—and they knew he could do it again. Ezekiel's model communicated that God's punishment was not over. They weren't getting home soon, and their friends and relatives in Jerusalem were facing a disastrous future. The model also communicated another frightening thought. Just as the pan separated Ezekiel from the city, God also was outside of the city—perhaps, as Christopher Wright suggests, God himself was Judah's real enemy.[2]

We are not told how Ezekiel's audience responded to this particular message. Perhaps some took his message to heart, but most would have questioned his sanity. So instead of preparing for the worst, they chose to believe the more positive message of the false prophets like Jeremiah's

1. Clements, *Ezekiel*, 22.
2. Wright, *The Message of Ezekiel*, 76.

nemesis, Hananiah, who was promising that the yoke of the king of Babylon would be broken and that the temple vessels, which Nebuchadnezzar had carried off to Babylon, would be returned together with King Jeconiah and all the exiles (Jer 28:2–4).

Ezekiel's unpopular street theatre performances continued. His second performance (vv. 4–8) resumed the theme of siege and was even more dramatic than the first. This time Ezekiel's action consisted of lying on his left side for 390 days and then on his right side for 40 days. The significance of these numbers is debated. One possibility is that the numbers added together represent the duration of the coming siege of Jerusalem. A second possibility is that the numbers correspond to the years of captivity of Israel and Judah. A third possibility is that the 390 days symbolize the four centuries of Israel's unremitting national sin beginning with the reign of Solomon and that the 40 days represent the 40 years that the generation of Jews already in exile would remain in exile. Though the significance of the numbers is somewhat ambiguous, the message is very clear and harsh. God had not finished judging his covenant-defying people. And judgement would go on for a very long time.

The third sign features a specially made bread and is perhaps the best known. Today, we find Ezekiel Bread in some specialty shops and find ads for it on the internet. One of these claims that Ezekiel Bread is "as healthy as bread gets" because it is "a type of sprouted bread, made from a variety of whole grains and legumes that have started germinating (sprouting)."[3] The recipe for the bread that God asks Ezekiel to make, however, is not presented as a healthy alternative for God's people living in Judah to

3. Gunnars, "Ezekiel Bread."

consume. On the contrary, the recipe produced a small eight-ounce loaf made with the only grains and legumes that were available in a time of siege. Ezekiel was to take wheat, barley, beans, lentils, millet, and spelt and put them together into a storage jar. Then, each day that he was lying on his side, he was to make a small loaf of bread and eat it and drink a little more than a one-half liter of water. This was a starvation diet. If this is all Ezekiel ate and drank during the day for 430 days, his community would have watched him grow thinner and thinner day by day. Ezekiel's tenacity either would have underscored people's opinion that he was nuts or would have pushed them to take his message seriously. Certainly when news of the fall of Jerusalem came to God's people in Babylon in 587, they all recognized that Ezekiel was a true prophet.

There is another part of this last sign act however that needs to be unpacked. Verse 12 of Ezekiel chapter 4 presents us with an interpretive challenge that is glossed over in most modern translations, which translate God's command to Ezekiel as follows: "You shall eat it [that is, the previously mentioned bread] as a barley cake, baking it in their sight on human dung" (Ezek 4:12, NRSV). The NIV translation reads similarly. The Hebrew, however, literally reads, "A barley cake, you shall eat it; and on bits of human excrement you shall bake it, as they watch you." Do these words present a second baking challenge for Ezekiel? Was he to make a barley cake in addition to the previously mentioned Ezekiel Bread? While this interpretation is possible, I suggest we follow the majority of translators and commentators and read this verse as God's further instructions about how to bake this unusual bread. This verse suggests that Ezekiel's small loaf was not simply to communicate something about the difficulty of life under

God's impending judgement, but it was to communicate something about uncleanness—it was to reveal to those who were sitting comfortably in Jerusalem that they would soon be living a nonkosher life in Babylon.

Ezekiel's outrage is not surprising. After all he was a priest as well as a prophet and was very sensitive to issues of ritual cleanliness. How could he possibly eat bread baked on human excrement?

Ezekiel protests, "Not so Sovereign LORD! I have never defiled myself. From my youth until now I have never eaten anything found dead or torn by animals. No unclean meat has ever entered my mouth" (Ezek 4:14). God's response to Ezekiel's pushback is somewhat surprising. He says, "Okay! I will let you bake your bread over cow manure instead of human excrement" (v. 15). Perhaps cooking on cow dung also sounds disgusting to those of us who are postmodern city dwellers. But we need to know that cow manure mixed with straw was a common fuel for cooking fires in the ancient world and is used in some places even today.

God's concession to Ezekiel's outrage means that the symbolic significance of this particular sign action was changed. The small multigrain and legume bread baked on cow dung together with the small drink of water Ezekiel had each day would now symbolize the shortage of food during the siege—it would not communicate the idea of uncleanness.

To conclude, the three acts of street theatre featured in Ezekiel chapter 4 were meant to communicate a specific message to God's people in exile. They were meant to hear that God's judgement of his people was not over; that God had not abandoned them in exile; that they were in Babylon for the long haul; and that they would soon be joined by God's people who were still living in Judah. The third sign act also became a teaching moment for God's prophet. Ezekiel was not willing to obey God's command to consume bread baked on human dung and he pushed back. God graciously heard his cry and changed the plan. God's empathetic response to his prophet showed Ezekiel that Israel's God was not only a holy God who had plans for his people but was also a God of empathy and compassion, one who listened to Ezekiel and understood his desire to remain ritually pure and so modified the message.

The message of this chapter however is not locked into the past. It continues to speak to us today. It reminds us first of all that sin has consequences. God did not tolerate the covenant breaking of his people in the past and he does not take sin lightly today. Secondly, this chapter invites us to consider God's call on our lives. Sometimes God calls us to do things that our culture, our friends, and even our families think are outrageous. We have three examples of such outrageous requests in this chapter and Ezekiel was willing to do almost all of them. When he did push back God listened, felt his pain, empathized with his prophet, and modified the recipe. This portrait of an empathetic, listening God reminds us of our great high priest Jesus, who empathizes with our weaknesses as Heb 4:15–16 reminds us. This reality gives us confidence to approach God's throne of grace with all our concerns, with our sense of being overwhelmed with what seems to us to be an impossible call, with our sense of dismay, with our outrage, and with our anger—because it is before God's throne of grace that we, like Ezekiel, find mercy and grace in our time of need.

Scripture: Ezekiel 4

Questions for Further Reflection

1. How do you think Ezekiel's audience responded to his street theatre?

2. What do these three sign acts tell us about Ezekiel as a person?

3. What does this chapter teach us about the character of God? Read Heb 4:15–16. Do you think the portrayal of God as an empathetic listener in our text from Ezekiel anticipates God's fuller revelation in Jesus Christ our great high priest in Hebrews 4?

4

No Other Place to Stand

EPHRAIM RADNER

EZEKIEL 5, AS IT turns out, does speak to a way in which I have come, more and more of late, to view the Christian life. But if there is an axe to be ground here, it is not mine; it is God's, and he is doing the grinding.

For an immediate question that this chapter raises with force is, where do we stand before this Word, that is God's word to us? It's a question that faces individuals, churches, and the church as a whole: is it ever possible to listen in, from the *outside*, as it were, to the roaring proclamation of God's judgment on sin? And Ezekiel 5 seems to answer: it is *not* possible; there is very *little* ground on which to stand *apart* from the sweeping force of God's work laid out by the prophet. What we hear instead is the exhaustive and absolute character of God's destructive judgment upon Israel—and that judgment, if we enter into the people's life as I believe is our duty and even our identity, engulfs us as well.

Let us listen to this carefully: Ezekiel is told to enact visibly the breadth of God's judgment on his people. With a sword, to cut off his hair and beard, and divide it up into three equal parts, reserving a bit to attach to the hem of his robe. Then, one by one each pile of his hair is to be destroyed—burning it, chopping it up, scattering it to the winds. Even those remaining hairs he has bound to his robe are to be thrown in the fire (Ezek 5:4). It is a symbolic drama meant to demonstrate the sheer comprehensiveness, the *allness* of Israel's destruction at the hand of God. All of Israel: killed by the Babylonians; strained and struck down by disease as they are squeezed by siege and then destitution and famine; taken away captive and into exile to the ends of the earth. 2 Kings, Jeremiah, or Lamentations give us the details. Even that little hair-on-the-hem, those few who survive this holocaust—perhaps representing Gedaliah left in the land, struggling, succumbing to assassination, plotting, allying themselves with others, in Egypt, in the desert, stragglers to divine condemnation, thinking they could escape the worst (see 2 Kings 25:22–26) . . . even these too are thrown, as we know, into the furnace or are mowed down like dried rushes before the sickle. Strategies and tactics simply consumed.

This is a frightening, and certainly overwhelming chapter. And it is designed just as Ezekiel's actions are ordered—or rather, *God's* actions are pursued—so as to shock, not just us, but the nations, the world itself: "I am going to do something that I have never done before, nor can it be conceived of again" (v. 9). God's judgment and its furiously exhaustive extent are almost annihilating—like a dammed up river, swollen by torrential rains, that finally bursts out and deluges the landscape and all living things in its path, "without pity" (v. 11) God announces, until, finally, as Ezekiel says, God's anger is "spent," finished, and like some madness, relieved (v. 13). Left behind is a people, Israel, whose humiliation and perversion is

complete—driven even to the horrific depths of canni-
balism in the famine-struck city of Jerusalem, something
Lamentations confirms (Lam 2:20; 4:10), with mothers
and fathers eating their dead children, children eating the
flesh of their dead parents (Ezek 5:10). Israel is debased
beyond even the twisted imagination of her enemies (vv.
6, 15).

In the face of this tempestuously inclusive divine destruction, then, where are we to stand? You are at the least,
with *me*, the prophet seems to say. With me. For at the
front end of the chapter is the figure of Ezekiel himself. It
is he who sets up the embodied nature of this horrendous
vista. Shaving head and beard; burning, cutting, scattering
the piles of his hair, his *own* hair. He stands for his own
people. In all this, Ezekiel is himself drawn in to the horror
of the unfolding present and future, not only as a specta-
tor, but as a participant. What he is asked to do by God,
understand, is itself a defilement, according to the Law. As
a priest (1:3), he is forbidden to shave his head (Lev. 21:5),
hair being perhaps a sign of divine life and creation, to be
removed only in mourning or in humiliation (cf. Deut
21:12; 2 Sam 10:4–5; Isa 7:20). As in the previous chapter,
Ezekiel is actually *made* by God to render himself impure,
like his people on whom God's condemnation is hurtling.
He is, after all, he and his family, already a part of that scattered hair of his, thrown in the blistering winds of captivity
in Babylon. He is an exiled prisoner, like the rest of them.
He already carries, that is, the burden of the judgment he
announces in his own body.

Bishop Stephen Andrews, in discussing chapters 2–3,
tells us that part of Ezekiel's word is to teach *us* our own
calling. Is *this* that calling? That the servants of God should
be consumed in their Master's own fire? That the righteous

should be expected to expire with the unrighteous? You can think about what this might mean, what contexts this could refer to. But whatever the case, if you think this is a justice problem, you are probably right. But it is a justice problem with *God* from the start, not with Ezekiel, not with Scripture. After all, God's absolute and exhaustive destructive judgment carries away with it, burns down with it, the good and bad together. It always has. Pastors, servants, the generous and wicked, in a single flood. Ask the people of Cambodia, Rwanda, Aleppo . . . and more. This is what God does, if there is a God.

And if this sounds shocking, it's because it *is* shocking. This very question opens Origen's commentary on Ezekiel, the first Christian commentary on the book that we know of. Ezekiel, Origen says, presents us with a tremendous moral challenge: this judgment, and *all* these people judged, and the fact that the righteous, like Ezekiel himself, are swallowed up in this judgment along with everyone else. And Origen wonders how such a message of the righteous swept away with the wicked can be good news. As well he might. He then answers at length, by saying, basically: it wasn't *their* fault; it wasn't Ezekiel's fault that he was taken away captive. It was, instead, an act of divine *mercy* for the righteous to suffer with sinners. Mercy, Origen insists: for the righteous provide "relief" (*subsidium*, in Jerome's Latin translation of Origen), as he puts it, to the wicked, simply by being there, in the midst of the wicked's self-destruction and demise. They provide relief by warning, by correcting and reproving; but also by just standing alongside, sharing, giving an example.[1] Ezekiel doesn't ever speak, in his whole book, of divine "love" except once, I think. But here it is, in a stark and costly

1. Origen, *Homily on Ezekiel* 1, 1.

form: the righteous mixed up with the unrighteous—bad things happening to good people, in the classic theodical quandary—because it is an act of God's mercy that the righteous and the unrighteous be put *together.*

And this, then, is a *divine* calling: joining the righteous to the act of God's exhaustive judging; and joining the righteous to those exhaustively judged. Friend of God the Judge, like Abraham (cf. Isa 41:8; Jas 2:23); and friend of the judged, friend of sinner also (Matt 11:19). A divine calling perfected only in one person, who "made his grave with the wicked . . . though he had done no violence" and was "without deceit" (Isa 53:9), becoming sin though he was without sin (2 Cor 5:21; cf. Gal 3:13). We know, you see, that in Christ somehow, this perfect joining of friend of the Judge and friend of the judged ends up being mercy, love, redemption itself. Somehow, by some miraculous confection of divine ingredients. I don't understand it; but I know it is *truthful,* that is, that it takes account of *all* the facts, including hope itself.

But to do that, the joining is absolutely critical in both directions: you can't have one without the other. If you want a cross without that—if you want a cross that is a kind of interposition between Judge and judged and not a joining of the two; a cross that is a buffer between them or an escape of one from the other, the righteous untouched by the wicked, the righteous silent in the face of wickedness—that is not what this is. And the people of Cambodia, Rwanda, and Aleppo will say, as will many of you, who may have a schizophrenic parent or broken siblings or lost children or rotten bodies—they and you will say in the face of such a cross, "that is *not* Ezekiel's cross, or Isaiah's cross, or Paul's . . . or Jesus's"—they and you will say to the purveyors of this other and this false cross, "you have ignored the world." If there is healing—and there *is*—it is where the righteous and wicked are thrown *together* into God's hands and where God delivers himself into theirs; where Truth speaks openly to evil; and yet where Truth stands immovably alongside it.

That is a perfect calling for Christ. But a calling nonetheless for us as well. He is friend of the Judge and friend of sinner. And Jesus calls us "his friends" also (John 15:14-15). For too long, for too many centuries, in too many dioceses and congregations, in too many ecclesial and cultural struggles, we have spurned a friendship such as this. Yet if we stand where Ezekiel stands—and there is no other place to stand for the righteous—we cannot run away; from Israel, from Babylon, from the long road between the two, from the words and reality of judgment, and from the hope given in standing beside the judged. Whatever our sense of purity and duty, prophecy and witness may be, there is only this one *place* in which any of this takes a living form.

Scripture: Ezekiel 5

Questions for Further Reflection:

1. What is the extent of God's judgment on Israel, as depicted by the prophet?

2. Should Christians or the Christian church identify with Israel in this case? With Ezekiel?

3. Why does the Christian church continue to read this text as "the Word of God"?

4. Does the cross of Christ illuminate or obscure the meaning of Ezekiel's words here?

5. To what situations of today might Ezekiel's description of God's judgment pertain, and how might the church situate itself in relation to them?

5

When Idolatry Infiltrates the Church

GLEN TAYLOR

THE DATE IS SEPTEMBER 18, 592 BC. A thirty-one-year-old prophet and priest—an eccentric man with wild eyes and a passion for God—is sitting in his house in Babylon. His former house in Jerusalem lay in ruins. Five years previously Ezekiel and his wife tasted firsthand what modern-day Syrian refugees are experiencing today. Their homeland has been levelled, pummelled by a war and the horrific things that go with it: the burning of people's homes, starvation, the ruthless killing of men, women, and children, and emigration. Once they lived in a beautiful city, where children laughed at play, and where streets buzzed with the hum of commerce. But now it's like a mass migration scene from the late-night news: dirt roads are filled with families fleeing the killing, carrying bags of belongings, and holding the hands of children whose eyes drip with tears and tell of fear. And in Ezekiel's case the enemy has not been left behind; rather it has become his new immigration officer who directs him to live in Babylon against his will and at the point of a spear. Like the Assyrians before them, the Babylonians kept the people of conquered countries from rebelling by deporting their leaders to a different country. Ezekiel and his wife no doubt felt like the psalmist who wrote:

> By the rivers of Babylon,
> There we sat down and wept,
> When we remembered Zion.
> Upon the willows in the midst of it
> We hung our harps.
> For there our captors demanded of us songs,
> And our tormentors mirth, saying,
> "Sing us one of the songs of Zion."
>
> How can we sing the LORD'S song
> In a foreign land?
> If I forget you, O Jerusalem,
> May my right hand forget her skill.
> May my tongue cleave to the roof of my mouth,
> If I do not remember you,
> If I do not exalt Jerusalem
> Above my chief joy. (Ps 137:1–6, NASB)

Like Ezekiel, some of you reading this essay are living away from home right now. As I recall from my own student days living abroad, that can be tough. I can imagine that you and Ezekiel have tried the same coping tactics, such as staying busy to keep your mind off events at home. And when good news of home comes through Face Time or Skype, it's great. It's good to know all is well in "God's country"—your homeland.

Ezekiel's Face Time with friends in Jerusalem, in the vision recounted in Ezekiel 8, is far from reassuring; it is in fact his (and God's) worst nightmare. And Ezekiel knows that he must share the grim news as a sort of personal lesson for the elders who have gathered in his house in Babylon.

Here's how the video session went. All at once, and literally in a flash, Ezekiel is taken up in a vision of God that included fire, gleaming metal, and a hand that grabbed him by the hair (Ezek 8:3).[1] God's spirit upholds him as it takes him to the temple in Jerusalem. But what he sees borders on obscenity.

The first scene takes place at the inner entrance to the northern gate of the temple. Ironically, this vista begins with what is normally a good thing: seeing the glory of God. But this sight instead occasions a shocking embarrassment, because beside the glory of God is what is called an "image of jealousy." As we know from the use of the special word for "image" here, it is almost certainly an image of the Canaanite goddess Asherah.[2] As offensive as that alone would be to God, in 1979 archaeologists found evidence that the situation was far worse; some Israelites understood the goddess Asherah as relating to God—as his wife![3] Moreover, when depicted this goddess is usually buck naked. It is no wonder, so God tells Ezekiel, that this image is utterly disdainful; it is a despicable affront to the glory of God. In fact it leads God to declare that he will soon leave his sanctuary in Jerusalem.

It's scary to think that God, having once left the temple, could perhaps also leave the church. Almost no one

1. Mesopotamian parallels attest to the practice of a god, also described as a shining figure, taking a key figure by the hair on a journey to the netherworld. Walton and Keener, *Cultural Backgrounds Study Bible*, 1343.

2. The Hebrew word is *semel*; compare 2 Kings 21:7 with 2 Chr 33:7, 15.

3. See conveniently Taylor, "Was Yahweh Worshiped as the Sun?" 52–61, 90–91.

before 586 BC believed that God would—even could—do this. But listen to what God says in verse 6. It is a lesson to Ezekiel and to the elders sitting in his house, who represent the people of God and who share in the guilt of this transgression; and indirectly it is a lesson to the leadership of his house, the church today: "And He said to me, 'Mortal, do you see what they are doing, the terrible abominations that the House of Israel is practicing here, to drive Me far from My Sanctuary?" (Ezek 8:6, NJPS)

Will God ever leave the church for its apostasy? I don't know; I'm not a theology professor. But let me ask: "Do *we* see what they are doing?" Let us take heart and learn from it. Because God is both holy and sovereign, no theological tenet framed by mere humans can trump the sovereign will of God.

Ezekiel is next taken to the entrance to the courtyard of the inner frame of the temple complex. Everything looks in order (and so it often does); but wait. There's a blotch on the wall near the entrance. It cakes over a secret entrance that leads to a basement area where there are murals of animals and bugs, and lots of other idols. And here, venerating images of animals and all sorts of other idols in little coves, there are "elders," the equivalent of clergy—not members of the congregation, but seventy senior clergy, students of theology, including Jaazaniah, the son of a pious family that helped promote the reforms of king Josiah (cf. 2 Kings 22:8-13). And these clerics are burning incense, not censing the altar, but murals of snakes, cockroaches, and baboons. This scene reads like a picture page from the Egyptian Book of the Dead.

"Do you see O mortal what they are committing in the dark, each one in his room of idols" says the Lord. And listen to their justification, which has a familiar ring to it when I think of our culture and even parts of the church: "The LORD does not see us; the LORD has forsaken the land." (Ezek 8:12, NRSV)

"Do *we* see?" What are we committing in the dark, each one in his or her room of idols?

How foolish it would be to think that God does not "see" what we do in secret. Our text implies it is even ironic. For who is it that gives Ezekiel a vision? Who asks Ezekiel if he can "see" what God is showing him in the darkness? God sees. And he is asking Ezekiel, and us as readers, if we see the things that God sees.

The next scene involves women, mourning as they presumably venerate the God Tammuz, an ancient Sumerian shepherd god. Whatever the rite involved, it especially caught the imagination of women, and specifically involved mourning rites. (cf. 8:14) One text from about 250 years later describes Tammuz's wife Ishtar weeping over her husband.[4] Many scholars think Tammuz journeyed to the netherworld and back and that this corresponded to the dry and fertile agricultural seasons respectively.[5]

Not long ago I and my wife (also an Old Testament scholar) heard a female colleague give a presentation on this scene at an academic conference. To our surprise, this scholar was upholding these women as a role model for women of Christian and Jewish faith today. Now I believe there are good, godly, faithful forms of feminism that redress wrongs that ought to be made right, but theological novelty of this sort is certainly not the way to do it! I thank God for godly, theologically orthodox feminists like Fleming Rutledge and my female colleagues at Wycliffe College. They are a gift to the church.

4. Kaiser and Garrett, *Archaeological Study Bible*, 1320.
5. Ibid.

"Do you see O mortal?" God asks in our text. I believe his Spirit asks of us: "Do we see?" Apostasy is abhorrent to God and a means of undermining the faith. But the absolute worst is yet to come—and so with it a powerful message.

Lastly Ezekiel sees twenty-five men (later identified as priests) who, quite literally, are turning their backs to the holy of holies; instead of worshipping Yahweh, they bow to the east, towards the sun (8:16). Shocking here is not the turning of their backs to God and "instead" to the sun; it is their turning to worship what they understood to be a tangible "form" of Yahweh—as the sun.[6] These worshippers had convinced themselves that worshipping the sun was not a pagan practice, but that it was venerating an icon of Yahweh in the form of the sun itself. So, as in the case of the Asherah in vv. 5–6, these worshippers had turned a pagan form of worship into an acceptably "orthodox" form of Yahweh worship. (Its acceptability is attested by its practice in the Jerusalem temple, for what happens there, as in a church cathedral, happens only with the approval of key leaders.)

I wonder if by now you have seen a parallel between the sins committed in the temple (a theological crime scene) and a foundational passage of Scripture that is addressed to God's covenant people. The parallel passage is in Deuteronomy where Moses says:

> 15 Since you saw no form when the LORD spoke to you at Horeb out of the fire, take care and watch yourselves closely, 16 so that you do not act corruptly by making an idol for yourselves, in the form of any figure—the likeness of male or female, 17 the likeness of any animal

---

6. For an in-depth study, see Taylor, *Yahweh and the Sun.*

that is on the earth, the likeness of any winged bird that flies in the air, 18 the likeness of anything that creeps on the ground, the likeness of any fish that is in the water under the earth. 19 And when you look up to the heavens and see the sun, the moon, and the stars, all the host of heaven, do not be led astray and bow down to them and serve them." (Deut 4:15–19) [7]

You might be saying to yourself: "I don't worship images of God, animals, or bugs." I expect that's true. But, as the climactic scene involving the sun illustrates, we humans are very good at rationalizing what we do. *We are good at finding ways to fit things from our culture that we admire into our "orthodox" ways of worship.* Now I don't know how you rationalize things. And I wish I understood even better how I make religious and ethical compromises. But, as someone with an expertise in Israelite sun worship, I have a good idea about how the sun worshippers rationalized their syncretism. It went something like this: The second commandment forbids us from making images of God; we didn't make the sun, God did! The sun-god Shamash in Mesopotamia was, like Yahweh, a god of justice and the giver of laws to his people. And on the day Joshua prayed for the Lord to give him extra time to defeat his enemies, who answered that prayer to "Yahweh"? The sun! And take today, September 18, 562 BC. At this time of year, the autumnal equinox, the rays of the early morning sun shine directly into the innermost part of the temple.

---

7. Compare v. 16 to the first scene of Ezekiel 8 involving the setting up of a female image (Ezek 8:5–6). Compare v. 18 to the second scene of Ezekiel 8 involving the veneration of portraits of animals (Ezek 8:7–13). And compare v. 19 to the fourth scene of Ezekiel 8 involving the worship of the sun (Ezek 8:16–17).

What wonderful testimony that the rays of the sun manifest the glory of Yahweh!

So, from the time of Joshua, through to the time of Ezekiel, and of the Qumran community, and on into the Byzantine period, some Israelites venerated the sun as though it were a God-given icon of Yahweh. (The cult of Tammuz was also persistent; it is thought to have been a lure for women from 2300 BC until as late as the tenth century AD!)[8]

So, how more specifically can we apply the sorry, syncretistic lesson of Ezekiel 8? There are some big-ticket items that qualify as syncretism and some small-ticket ones that are trickier to negotiate for not being so clear. What are the big-ticket items? Here is a sampling of beliefs: that Jesus is not God incarnate, that Jesus is but one of many ways to God, that all religions are essentially the same, that God is now known to be too nice to get hung up about sin (sin being, after all, an unhealthy vestige of the Victorian era or the like). And, though it might not be syncretistic in itself, the apostate belief that we in the twenty-first century can no longer take the Bible seriously—at least to the point of doing what it actually says—opens a wide door of relativism that welcomes syncretism if only for having no longer any basis for judging what is syncretistic or not. Another symptom of syncretism is when churches remove the Nicene or Apostles' Creed from their liturgies.

What, then, about the small-ticket items? Take for example, the genuine need for the church today to make the gospel accessible to our culture, which is largely post-Christian, and which calls for adaptation. *Acceptable* adaptation requires real discernment.

---

8. Kaiser and Garrett, *Archaeological Study Bible*, 1321.

Before considering faithful discernment, let's be clear about what we mean by syncretism here. I like the following definition: "Syncretism, in this case, is the mixing of something else with Christianity such that it becomes a different gospel."[9]

There is a fine line between two extremes. On the one hand, there is *obscurantism*, which, in saying "don't change anything"—things like outdated hymns, and organ-only church music—unnecessarily prevents people in our culture from hearing and embracing the gospel. On the other hand, there is *syncretism*, which, in saying "change most anything and everything"—things like the creed, confession of sin, the cross and the atoning sacrifice of Jesus—risks injecting irreconcilable aspects of the culture into the gospel, thereby changing it into something different from the gospel itself, but deceptively similar to it. That is the danger. Making necessary adjustments that don't compromise the apostolic gospel is a big challenge.

A Russian parable illustrates the dilemma. A hunter is just about to pull the trigger on a bear, when the bear says soothingly, "Isn't it better to talk? What is it that you want? We can negotiate." The hunter lowers his gun and says, "I need a fur coat to keep me warm." The bear in turn says, "I'm simply foraging for a meal." In the end, the bear walks away alone, with the hunter nowhere in sight. The bear got a full belly. And the hunter got his wish too; for he is now surrounded by a coat of bear skin that is keeping him warm.[10]

9. Stetzer, "Avoiding the Pitfall of Syncretism." He adds: "Syncretism takes place with a positive-thinking gospel, a nationalist emphasis, or emerging culture. Syncretism happens more than we might know." This author also makes reference to the opposite polls of "obscurantism" and "syncretism."

10. Green, *Illustrations for Biblical Preaching*, 76.

Let me put God's question to Ezekiel generically: "Do we see the sorts of things that offend God?" Even more personally, let me ask a question that I ask of myself: "What sorts of sordid things might we be doing, banking on the notion that God does not see or, if he does, does not care, or relying on the belief that God will not or even cannot leave us?"

Quite some time ago a theology student that I taught was found out for his addiction to child pornography, an addiction he secretly fed from the privacy of his seminary dorm room. In what ways might we also be acting and thinking in ways that are at odds with the revealed will of God in Scripture and that affront the glory of God?

And if that sounds like a moralistic question from an Old Testament professor, recall that the New Testament doesn't cut us any more slack. As Paul says in 1 Corinthians, "Therefore, my dear friends, flee from the worship of idols." (10:14) And further, in 10:21–22 he reminds us: "You cannot drink the cup of the Lord and the cup of demons. You cannot partake of the table of the Lord and the table of demons. Or are we provoking the Lord to jealousy?"

Ezekiel's words are as relevant today as they were in the sixth century BC. And that's hardly a surprise. After all, his situation wasn't all that different from ours. As one writer puts it: "*His religion was very much a minority one, struggling to survive in a pluralist, multi-cultural society. The powerful country where he was exiled had many gods and he had only one. Yet he firmly proclaimed the message that there was one God, who would ultimately save his people, regardless of what other nations might do.*"[11] By God's grace let us together commit ourselves to remain

11. Carson et al., *New Bible Commentary*, 716 (emphasis mine).

true to the gospel in our day, to God's glory—a glory that one day decided enough was enough and left. ?

Scripture: Ezekiel 8

Questions for Further Reflection:

1. What are some other big-ticket examples of idolatrous practices today?

2. What do you think led the Israelites to engage in such blatant idolatry? What leads us to practices of idolatry today?

3. How is your church coping with the need for change in order to reach the culture of today with the message of the gospel? Do you lean more towards the obscurantist side of changing nothing, or the syncretistic side of accommodating too much? And how will you decide what is too little change and what is too much?

6

When God's Glory Leaves his People

PETER ROBINSON

*"Holy, Holy, Holy, is the Lord God of Hosts.
The whole earth is full of his Glory."*

—ISA 6:3

EZEKIEL'S VISION IN CHAPTER 10 brings to a climax the judgment of God on his people with the departure of his glory, of his presence, from the temple. As brutal as the vision of slaughter in chapter 9 is, with bodies piling up in the courts of the temple (Ezek 9:7–8) followed by burning coals of judgment (10:2), the vision of the departure of the glory of God signals the end to all hope for those left in Jerusalem.

This scene opens in chapter 8 with Ezekiel sitting in his house in Babylon and the elders of Judah gathered around him. They have come for a prophetic word from the Lord—but not this kind of word. They wanted a word that God was going to rescue them and return them to

Jerusalem: a word of hope in the midst of their experience of exile. Not this word of judgment.

Ezekiel is caught up by the Lord in this vision, just as he was in chapter 1, but now, a year or so later, everything becomes that much clearer. The elements that were shrouded or veiled in the first vision come into focus. Instead of sitting on the banks of the river Chebar, Ezekiel is carried by the Spirit of the Lord into the temple in Jerusalem (8:3). Ezekiel sees that the living creatures, from his first vision (cf. 1:4–14), are indeed the cherubim—figures familiar from the temple. Although, these are not the same as the carved figures in the temple because they are not simply representative figures, shaped by human hands. They are the real living cherubim, the ones who attend to God in his presence (cf. 10:1–5, 15–16).

In Ezekiel's vision in chapter 10, the cherubim, the sapphire throne, the clouds and bright splendor cry out the glory of God. The sound of the cherubim's wings fills the temple, even to the outer court, like the thunder of God's voice when he speaks (10:5). This thundering of God's voice seems to echo Ps 29:5 when the voice of God breaks or snaps the cedars of Lebanon, the same cedars that the temple is built with. Ezekiel is being assaulted on every front with the glory of God: thundering sound, shining light, burning heat. One can almost feel the foundations of the temple shudder. But there is no description of Ezekiel's response. The focus is wholly on God. This is the transcendent God, the holy, awesome, terrible God: "Holy, Holy, Holy is the Lord God of hosts." Here Ezekiel's vision more closely aligns with Isaiah's vision of the glory of God (cf. Isa 6:1ff.) than his earlier vision in Ezekiel chapter 1. Although, unlike Isaiah's vision, the burning coals Ezekiel sees are scattered in judgment (Ezek 10:2) rather than purifying the prophet to speak God's words.

God is judging the people for their abominations. "Then he [God] said to me, Son of man, do you see what they are doing, the great abominations that the house of Israel are committing here, to drive me far from my sanctuary?" (Ezek 8:6). Their abominations include syncretism and idolatry. But, lest we see their rebellious actions as God's primary concern, it is made clear that they are being judged because they are living as though God is not present.[1] Living as though God does not know what is going on. "Son of man, have you seen what the elders of the house of Israel are doing in the dark, each in his room of images? For they say, 'the Lord does not see us, the Lord has forsaken this land (8:12).'" This is repeated again in Ezek 9:9 in the midst of God's judgement: "For they say the Lord has forsaken the land and the Lord does not see." They have judged the Lord and found God wanting and that is all the justification they need for doing exactly what they want to do instead of obeying God.

Which brings us to the stark paradox: the cherubim who in Ezekiel 10 come to escort the glory of the Lord from the temple confirm that God has been present all along. This theophany is not the sudden appearance of a God who has long been absent, one who dwells in an altogether different space. No, God has been present in the temple the whole time, just as he had promised. God through his glory, his *kabod*, has been present in the temple while the elders or leaders of the people are sitting in the dark, oblivious to the presence of God, each in their room full of images or idols. All the while saying to themselves: "the Lord doesn't see us, the Lord left here a long time ago." The

1. See Jenson, *Ezekiel*, 85.

narrator allows us, along with Ezekiel, to look in on this scene and ask how can these elders not be aware? How can they ignore the holy transcendent God? "And this is judgment, that the light has come into the world, and people loved darkness rather than light because their deeds were evil." (John 3:19) Jerome, in his interpretation of this passage, sees it as marking the shift from Israel to the church.[2] The Lord is judging the people of Israel and his departure from the temple marks the end of God's commitment to Israel and a new beginning with the church. This Supersessionism, to our shame, has a long and appalling history in the church. We have been, to one extent or another, dealing with the fallout of this kind of interpretation ever since. What is perhaps most sobering for us today is how quickly we are able to see this as God's judgment of Israel and not God's judgment on us all. "Thank God that we are not like that," we say as we quickly move on to a more congenial topic. What should, of course strike us, is that Ezekiel's vision seems eerily prescient for our time. The refrain that plays continually in the background to our lives goes, "The Lord has forsaken us, the Lord does not see."

In his book *A Secular Age,* Charles Taylor speaks of the marks of this age. Central to the secular understanding, the way people inhabit this world, is that they live as though God isn't here at all. People have constructed and live with an understanding of the world that makes no provision for any authority outside the self. They may have gods or idols, indeed there are many to choose from. But these idols are part and parcel of our world, and they are strangely amenable to what people already value or hold dear. What is particularly sobering, is that this is true not

2. Jerome, *Letter 108*, 12–13

just of the world around us, it is true of us all in one degree or another.

In the church this takes the form of practical atheism. Unlike atheists, who declare there is no God, we in the church, like the elders in Jerusalem, too often claim to worship God while living day to day as though there is no God or as though God were too distant from the world to make any real difference. We either demythologize Jesus while assuming that we are just being honest and that we have to figure things out for ourselves, or we spiritualize Jesus while stressing our commitment to faithfulness. But the Jesus we are committed to is a little too tame and a little too manageable to line up with the Jesus who brings into focus the God of Scripture. Clinging fiercely to what we see as honesty or faithfulness, we fail to recognize that we, like the elders of Israel, are sitting in the dark with our own images or idols.

Another problem with seeing this passage through a Supersessionist lens and as no longer applicable for the church today is that this robs us of true hope in a faithful God. Throughout Ezekiel we have repeated reminders that God, the holy transcendent other, does not dwell in an altogether separate space. No this God, in a multitude of different ways, makes himself present and active in our world. This is evident in Ezekiel's first vision when God's glory appears to him while he is on the banks of the Chebar river. And it continues when God comes to Ezekiel in Babylon. God is present even in exile. God's glory, God's presence in the world is not limited to the temple even though the temple is essential to God's taking form and shape in the world. The declaration of a God who consistently shows up and consistently acts culminates in Ezekiel 43 when the glory of the Lord returns to the eschatological temple through the same east gate from which God had departed. And from our New Testament vantage point, we know this eschatological temple to be the person of Jesus Christ. (cf. John 2:19). This central truth of our faith finally exposes the lie to our claim that "the Lord is not here; the Lord does not see." The issue is not whether God is present in our space and time or whether God will show up. It is the other way around—our space and time only exist because of God's faithful sustaining of them.

All of this points us towards the cross as the place where the depths and riches of God's faithfulness are unveiled. Together with Isaiah 6 and Ezekiel 10, John's gospel ties this together when John points to Christ lifted up as the revelation of the glory of God—"Father, the hour has come; glorify your son that he may glorify you." (John 17:1) If we believe that God gave up on the people of Israel because of their unfaithfulness then we have missed the heart of the gospel which is that, even in the face of the most consistent human rebellion against God, God continues to work for our redemption. Indeed, the true character and glory of God are revealed in the midst of human rebellion. The cross can only be understood in the light of God's unyielding faithfulness to Israel.

May we, in the church today, allow God to open our eyes that we may see his glory: *Holy, Holy, Holy, is the Lord God of Hosts. The whole earth is full of his Glory.*

Scripture: Ezekiel 9–10

Questions for Further Reflection:

1. In what ways do we, in the church, live as though God is not present and does not hear us (practical

atheism)? What are some of the ways in which we might cultivate a sense of attentiveness to God?

2. At certain points in the church's history, Supersessionism has encouraged a low view of the Jewish people and of the Jewish faith. What are some ways in which this kind of thinking distorts our understanding of the Christian faith?

3. While the book of Ezekiel speaks clearly of the judgement of God there is, alongside of that, an underlying foundation of the unshakeable faithfulness of God. How can this alignment of faithfulness and judgment help us more clearly see God's heart for the world?

7

Waking from the Amnesia of Infidelity

KIRA MOOLMAN

WHEN I WAS FIRST asked to write for this series, I was incredibly honored. When I read what the chapter would be, I thought about saying no because I was too busy. I was too intimidated by the passage. Saying no was the first temptation. The second temptation was to write only on the first part of Ezekiel chapter 16: the recovered orphan, the "foundling bride." I thought we could linger here, delineate those Ruth overtones of God spreading his garment over a vulnerable woman (cf. Ezek 16:8). We would end our reading at verse 14:

> "Your fame spread among the nations on account of your beauty,
>
> for it was perfect because of my splendor that I had bestowed on you, says the Lord God." (NRSV)

This temptation dangled in front of me to do what we often do in church: completely skip over the ugly parts, do our best to keep people from squirming in the pews or sweating in the pulpit.

I thought I had conquered all temptation once I settled on reading the verses we read today—but soon found myself ensnared in a third. You see, the more time I spent in the text, the more I wanted to somehow make the unpalatable palatable. I kept looking for help in commentaries, ways to excuse the imagery. How could I make sure that you, the reader, did not finish this meditation thinking of God as destructive and abusive? How could I make sure that we did not have these lingering images of a personified Jerusalem stripped bare, stoned, and pierced with swords?

Maybe it would help if we thought of Ezekiel's audience. Those hearing him would have mostly been men, who would have found it abhorrent to be compared to a woman, let alone this whoring woman.[1] Or could it help if we spoke of Ezekiel's context, of living in the blank trauma after exile, the life of vacant stares? Could we see these were people that needed to be shocked into attention?[2] I grasped at ways to turn the passage on its head, to find a way to make it easier to swallow.

I wondered, "Would the reader feel more comfortable if I apologized? Would it make it better to say that God is not human, that his jealousy is the only jealousy that makes sense, and that this passage does not give humans permission to meet infidelity with violence?"[3]

Maybe all those attempts and caveats do help a little. And they are important to say. But focusing only on this

1. Taylor, "Ezekiel," 407.

2. Such use of trauma studies and the need for shocking rhetoric is described in Lapsley, "Ezekiel," 288.

3. One concern from feminist scholars has been that the violence that meets Israel's infidelity would give justification for domestic abuse. See Lapsley, "Ezekiel," 288.

means that we still end up skipping over the text: that old temptation.

There is a precedence for this. In the history of its existence this chapter has often been banned from public reading.[4] So, like much of the tradition, we do not find ourselves at home here and rightly so. Ezekiel does not spend time crafting these brutal images so that we can explain them away, defang them, smooth them over.

Things started off so well. We first hear a story of God taking an abandoned orphan, caring for her, making her his very own and lavishing her with his name, with his honor, and with his gifts (Ezek 16:8–14). In this chapter Ezekiel takes on the metaphor of Hosea: the faithful God as husband and his unfaithful people as wife. And then Ezekiel turns the tap to full blast, scalding his hearers both then and now. For Jerusalem has not just been unfaithful; Ezekiel tells us she has prostituted herself. A lot. He does not play a subtle game. Though translations echo our attempts to make the text less offensive, we are told Jerusalem builds a platform on every street corner and spreads her legs to every passerby (v.25).[5]

Ezekiel piles up such images: Jerusalem fashions idols for herself and fornicates with what she has made (v.17). She does not get paid for her sexual favors—she bribes others to sleep with her (vv. 18–19). She uses the gifts God gave her for these bribes (v.33-34). And she sacrifices her own children in the process. Verses 20 and 21 accuse further:

> "You took your sons and your daughters, whom
> you had borne to me, and these you sacrificed
> to them [your idols] to be devoured. As if your

4. See Stiebert, *The Exile and the Prophet's Wife*, 19.
5. Taylor, "Ezekiel," 407.

whorings were not enough! You slaughtered my children and delivered them up as an offering to them [your idols]."

With this vivid and violent language, Ezekiel blurs lines between allegory and actuality. For we know that ancient Israel was surrounded by religions that included child sacrifice and systematic prostitution of its female worshippers, where altars became beds of fornication.[6] The implication of idolatry here is not just a metaphor then, for to serve the gods of other peoples meant that Israel followed their practices: prostitution and child sacrifice.

This meant perverting the blessings that God had promised to his people Israel: that her descendants would be numerous and she would be a light to the nations. The locus of blessing in offspring and fertility became twisted. In her idolatry, prostitution, and sacrifice of her children, in following those around her instead of her God, Israel smothered her light and her blessings.

And all of this because she forgot her God. This chapter is the reminder needed by a people so accustomed to their infidelity that they no longer notice it. With these words Ezekiel puts his hands on Jerusalem's shoulders and shakes. Hard. Wake up!

Thus, verse 22 continues, "In all your abominations and your whorings you did not remember the days of your youth, when you were naked and bare, flailing about in your blood." This is the old sin, the basic sin that Israel is so often accused: "You forgot; you did not remember." Israel does not just forget what has happened—but who God is. "I was the one who brought you out of slavery," God cries. "I was the one who taught you how to walk!" (cf. Hos 11:3)

6. As Jenson describes in his commentary. See Jenson, *Ezekiel*, 130.

Here too, Israel's beauty is "perfect because of my splendor that I had bestowed on you" (Ezek 16:14) God says, but all of this is forgotten by the faithless people.

And then, following this, we hear depictions of fierce, violent, and abusive judgment: "I will judge you as women who commit adultery and shed blood are judged, and bring blood upon you in wrath and jealousy" (v.38). We see in our reading what that looks like: nakedness, stones, swords; Israel bruised and bloody and broken. It is not easy to hear.

We cannot fall into the temptation of excusing the text away. It is, of course, a hard text to get through. But it is not finished either. At the end of the chapter God binds himself to Israel once more, promising an everlasting covenant (Ezek 16:59-60, 62-63). He knows Israel is not going to pull her weight. She will be sucked into idolatry again and again; she will forget, again and again. She will fall into that amnesia of infidelity. But this is not a covenant of equals; it is not a marriage of humans. This is a covenant between the true God and his people.

God makes a promise to himself to bind himself to Israel, to remain faithful despite her infidelity. And he follows through on it: he follows through to the point of nakedness and swords, his own body bruised and bloody and broken for us. This is the cost of unfaithfulness. And God pays it. He asks Israel—and us—to remember who he is: He is the God who chose his people when *they* were lost and alone, naked and vulnerable. He is the God who *himself* is born as a child, naked and vulnerable. He is the God who stays faithful in the face of temptation, and the God who is stripped and pierced that we might be his bride. So thanks be to that God and for his blood, blood that continues to cover all our everyday infidelities.

Scripture: Ezekiel 16

Questions for Further Reflection:

1. Read through Ezekiel 16. Imagine being in the room when Ezekiel shared this prophetic word with Israel. What do you think might be going through your head? What does the room feel like? Are people muttering and fidgeting, or is the room quiet and tense? How can you imagine people responding?

2. Have you ever heard this passage read in your church? Why do you think it is difficult for us to talk about passages like this in church? How would you describe it (shocking, vulgar, unnecessary, effective, etc.)? Do you think this passage should be read in church? Why or why not?

3. This meditation ends by finding Jesus reflected in Ezekiel 16, as the one who takes the place of unfaithful Israel and paying the price for its infidelity. Read through the passage again with Jesus in mind. Do any other passages of Scripture come to mind? Compare Ezekiel 16 and Isaiah 53. Where might they overlap or differ?

4. How does Ezekiel 16 lead you to pray? How can we pray for faithfulness for ourselves and each other?

8

Consider, Turn, and Live

ANDREW C. WITT

THE BOOK OF EZEKIEL is quite stark and frank about the impending doom to be unleashed upon the inhabitants of Jerusalem. Indeed, not merely the prophet Ezekiel, but Jeremiah, Zephaniah, and other prophets are all unmistakably clear: the people of Israel, the LORD's chosen and covenant people, have broken their vows; they have broken faith, they have forsaken their God, their only place of hope, and have given their thoughts, words, and deeds—indeed their very trust—over to the idols of the nations around them.

The figures and images used by Ezekiel to make clear to Israel its unfaithfulness are often grotesque, disturbing, brutal, and for some, irredeemably problematic. Ezekiel 18 does not contain any of those images. Although, while its words are more plain and transparent, the message that it brings to us is designed to cut into us deeply. Like a double-edged sword reaching into bone and marrow, its aim is to awaken us from our slumber, to challenge our presumptions, and reduce to nothing any pretense of fatalism that might lead to apathy.

The text itself is situated within several prophetic messages in chapters 12–19 which are related to the destruction and captivity of the city of Jerusalem, focusing in on popular proverbial statements during these trying and desperate times (cf. Ezek 12:22–23).

And make no mistake, this coming destruction is inevitable. There is nothing that anyone can do about it. Given this context, it is important to see what may have led to the proverbial statements found in Ezek 18, statements expressing the people's resignation and apathy.

Second Kings is greatly helpful in this regard. In that book, the law of Moses, neglected for many years, is rediscovered during Josiah's reign. King Josiah and the other leaders read it and are quite disturbed by the punishments for disobedience they find there. They conclude, "Great is the wrath of the Lord that is kindled against us, because our ancestors did not obey the words of this book, to do according to all that is written concerning us" (2 Kgs 22:13). So they send for the prophet Huldah, in part, I think, to make sure that they are reading these texts correctly, and perhaps hoping that she might relay to them words of hope. Not today. We read in 2 Kgs 22:16–17:

> 16 Thus says the Lord, I will indeed bring disaster on this place and on its inhabitants—all the words of the book that the king of Judah has read. 17 Because they have abandoned me and have made offerings to other gods, so that they have provoked me to anger with all the work of their hands, therefore my wrath will be kindled against this place, and it will not be quenched.

Holding out hope, even still, Josiah attempts to clean house through reform. He calls for the removal of idols from the high places throughout Judah and Samaria, restores the temple, and holds the Feast of Passover for the entire nation. Everyone is involved, and perhaps even a shift in momentum was perceived on the ground. Perhaps judgement was not imminent. But Huldah's message was not veiled: "Still the Lord did not turn from the fierceness of his great wrath, by which his anger was kindled against Judah, because of all the provocations with which Manasseh had provoked him" (23:26).

Think of the despair this message would have conveyed. What hope does the current generation have when they have already passed the point of no return? Why even attempt to be faithful? Why not be resigned to fate, and do what is right in our own eyes? What difference will any of it make? So we get the proverb that became commonplace throughout Israel, the proverb which opens Ezek 18, "The fathers have eaten sour grapes, and the children's teeth are set on edge" (18:2). Or, as the book of Lamentations puts it, "Our fathers have sinned, and are no more; and we bear their iniquities" (Lam 5:7).

For Ezekiel this proverb speaks to the desperation and despair that he encountered from those who had already gone into exile. They believed that "the son suffers for the iniquity of the father" (Ezek 18:19), and by implication, that "the ways of the LORD are unjust" (18:25, 29). Now, the Mosaic law is quite clear that punishment for generational sin within the family only proceeds across generations of those who hate God (Exod 20:5–6; 34:6–7). However, the root of the proverb in our text appears to be the belief that people are being punished corporately and generationally for the sins of their ancestors: "We bear their iniquities." Why should their generation suffer for the unbelief and sins of former generations?

Ezekiel, however, is having none of it. His counter-message is concise and cuts to the point, "Know that all lives are mine; the life of the parent as well as the life of the child is mine: it is only the person who sins that shall die" (Ezek 18:4). And in case that isn't clear enough, he illustrates his point by walking through three generations of a family. You have a righteous father, who does what is lawful and just, who follows the laws of the LORD—he shall surely live (vv. 5–9). You then have his son, a violent murderer, who acts contrary to the laws of the LORD—he will surely die, despite his father being righteous (vv. 10–13). And, finally, you have a grandson, who looks at the ways of his father, considers them, and chooses not to follow in his footsteps. Despite his father's sins, the grandson will live while his father will die (vv. 14–18). The point is plain and simple: "The person who sins shall die. A child shall not suffer for the iniquity of a parent, nor a parent suffer for the iniquity of a child; the righteousness of the righteous shall be his own, and the wickedness of the wicked shall be his own" (v. 20). Because God is righteous, we are all judged individually on our own merits. This in itself is just and right.

But notice that Ezekiel does not stop here. He takes things a step further and shows us that God is more than just in his righteousness: he is a God who offers mercy and grace for those who deserve to die. So we read, "If the wicked turn away from all their sins that they have committed and keep all my statutes and do what is lawful and right, they shall surely live; they shall not die. None of the transgressions that they have committed shall be remembered against them; for the righteousness that they have done they shall live" (vv. 21–22). Our end is not determined by our past actions. This means that the unrighteous have opportunity to repent, to turn from their sins towards God, towards righteousness. So says God, "Have I any pleasure in the death of the wicked, and not rather that they should turn from their ways and live?" (v. 23). We are not prisoners of our pasts, nor are we captive to the sins of others. Ezekiel is giving us a gloriously free and unqualified call to repentance and a new beginning.[1]

The repeated implication at the heart of the chapter is that today, at this time, God has given us the chance to consider the sins of former generations—and even our own—to consider the unrighteousness in our own lives: to consider them, to turn away from the wickedness we find, and to not do likewise. So, we must consider the ways in which we are like the people of Israel. Does God care about what might be stale, presumptuous traditions? What about our mechanically memorized statements of faith, or our pleasant smiles and friendly sayings of peace? Or what about our obligatory confessions of sin put on repeat without any real change? Just like God's people of old at his temple in Jerusalem, our own rituals and traditions have a real danger of becoming meaningless apart from trusting hearts which are turned towards God, coming to fruition in righteous deeds. Have you come to presume that your mere practice of ritual secures your relationship with Christ? As Ezekiel encourages us, we can "cast away" from ourselves all the transgressions we have committed and get for ourselves "a new heart and a new spirit" (cf., 18:31).

Later in the book, Ezekiel will put forward the LORD's vision of a *new* covenant which he is preparing for us, a covenant in which God himself will provide the new heart and new spirit to live before him and before each other (cf., Ezek 36:26–28 and 37:26–27). Ezekiel isn't alone in this

---

1. Clements, *Ezekiel*, 80-81.

vision. He joins Moses, Jeremiah, and Joel, as well as all of the people of faith which we read about in the Scriptures (cf., Deut 30:6; Jer 31:31–33; and Joel 2:28–29)—they all longed for and hoped for our days, when the veil to the Holy of Holies has been torn aside, where we can boldly approach the very throne of the LORD, and make our claim to the realities of the new covenant, purchased by the broken body and poured-out blood of Jesus Christ (cf., Heb 10:19–22). While today is still called today, we are invited to turn away from lethargy and apathy, from sulking in the doom of fatalistic thinking. Our end is not determined by past actions, whether from previous generations or our own. Let us, then, come to Jesus, the author and perfecter of our faith. Let us approach the throne of grace, where he willingly and freely gives aid to those who would but ask for it. Let us be the people who heed Ezekiel's exhortation to consider, to turn, and to live.

Scripture: Ezekiel 18

Questions for Further Reflection:

1. Can you think of any proverbial statements that have made their way into the church today which might not have biblical grounding? How might a prophet like Ezekiel have responded to that proverb?

2. Why does God care about the heart behind our traditions or rituals? What in your own practice of Christianity has become mere ritual or tradition?

3. Have you ever boldly claimed the new heart and spirit promised to you in the new covenant?

9

Exilic Revisionism

Ezekiel Revisits Israel's Founding Story

DAVID KUPP

WE ALL HAVE FOUNDING stories, those core myths that anchor our lives, our clans, our faith, our nation. We carry those stories with us wherever we go, an obligatory rucksack of narratives that shape our worldview. Let me recount one of my own founding stories.

It was May, 1980—less than a week before our wedding, in Spokane, WA. Late Sunday morning my fiancée and I went for a leisurely jog in the countryside after church. It was a sunny, fragrant spring morning (the very sort of day we dream of midwinter), and my soon-to-be-mother-in-law was probably happy to have me out of a very busy house.

Ellen and I reached the end of the country road, turned to jog back home, and stopped dead in our tracks. It was immediately apparent that the world was coming to an end. Looking up, the ancient "dome of heaven" now formed a solid, black shield, sliding rapidly from the west towards the eastern horizon, shutting off the sky and sun. The lid of the universe was closing above us, in startling, heart-stopping fashion. It was not quite noon, and within minutes it became dark as night. The street lights turned on; the birds stopped singing; the dog stood still and silent. And then the sky started to fall—black and grey pebbles, sand, and dust raining down. By the time we reached the house, the visibility had dropped to zero; breathing was nearly impossible.

It had taken 1,901 years, but in emergency radio broadcasts we learned that Pompei had arrived in the state of Washington. The largest volcanic eruption in American history had just hit the Pacific Northwest—it pulverized the top five hundred meters of Mount St. Helens. The plume of fire and ash rose twenty-four kilometers into the atmosphere, circled the earth, and dumped its residue in eleven states and five provinces. Dozens of people died. Wildlife, crops, forests, fisheries, and waterways were destroyed in the blast or buried in the ash, avalanches, and floods. Emergency declarations closed the roads and highways and airports; driving and flying was banned. The Canada-US border was barred and locked.

Our wedding had been dramatically upstaged. So the premise of our Ericson-Kupp founding myth could have been that weddings are, literally, a disaster!

However, the option to cancel our wedding was promptly vetoed by Ellen. "I've waited long enough," she declared. As the week wound towards Saturday, the emergency declaration began to ease, and the roads, airport, and border reopened just hours before the wedding. Picture a wedding chapel surrounded by grey, billowing clouds of ash and everyone in dust masks. The wedding party wore grey (not by choice). For the two of us this disaster narrative created a founding story about resilience: that <u>every natural and human catastrophe may generate suffering, but also opportunities for deeper</u> and richer community. For Ellen and I, that disaster narrative built solidarity and a new level of joy, laughter, and close, lifelong ties with those neighbors, family, and friends that endured much to gather and support us.

We live by our clan's founding stories and also by our national founding stories. These are the epics we tell each other at school, in church, in our homes, at public events, and through our official holidays. They provide the storyboard of how we became who we are, culturally, militarily, politically.

Grand *failures*, however, do not always reappear in grand narratives. <u>And over the years, we tend to sweeten our narratives.</u> So, challenging any founding story is a sensitive affair. For example:

- Think about Canada's grand story of the Underground Railway and the rescuing of slaves from the South—the telling of that epic rarely mentions Canada's own history of slavery.
- Think about our grand story of Canadian Confederation—the recitation of that narrative for decades did not include the Indian Act and Residential Schools.

Every nation and culture has these founding myths, which may leave out a critical part of the story. They often are woven together with a thread of exceptionalism.

Ezekiel fundamentally challenges and reshapes Israel's founding story in chapter 20 of the Book of Ezekiel. How and why does he do this?

Ezekiel delivers his speech in this chapter on August 14, 591 BCE. This is a year since the vision in the temple and two years after his initial call. The city of Jerusalem is still standing, and it seems that among the exiles a high level of optimism still prevails. Ezekiel is convinced that their optimism is naïve.

Once again (as in chapter 14) the elders of Israel in exile enter the prophet's house, and this time they probably hope for something more encouraging than his excoriations to date. They are profoundly disappointed, for in chapter 20 they find themselves on trial. Ezekiel turns the story of God and Israel into a prosecution speech. He "is commanded, in courtroom language, to *judge them* and *confront them* (20:4)."[1]

Ezekiel 16, 20 and 23 build toward the same purpose. Ezekiel's intention is to revisit the story of *YHWH's* people, in order to revise, reshape, and retell it through a revisionist lens. However, in a shift from the explicit, violent, lewd, and painful allegories of Ezekiel 16 and 23, he follows the same intent in chapter 20, but without allegorical device.

By the end of Ezekiel 20 three of Israel's fundamental religious and historical assumptions from the late monarchy will be deconstructed and shattered:

> that Israel could not be destroyed;
> that Jerusalem could not be violated;
> that the covenant could not be broken.

Ezekiel accomplishes this by tracing a new revisionary history across four periods of Israel's life:

1. Israel in Egypt

2. The first generation after the exodus

3. The second generation in the wilderness

1. Wright, *The Message of Ezekiel*, 157.

4. The years in the land up to and including the exile

These four periods of Ezekiel's history lesson are woven together with a four-part action sequence. Wright handily captures this (p.157), as adapted here:

Period Action	1. Israel in Egypt 20:5-9	2. Wilder-ness: 1st generation 20:10-17	3. Wilder-ness: 2nd generation 20:18-26	4. Conquest to exile 20:27-31
YHWH declares or acts graciously	vv.5-7	vv.10-12	vv.18-20	v.28a
But . . . Israel rebels	v.8a	v.13a	v.21a	v.28b
So . . . *YHWH's* anger declared and the people's destruction	v.8b	v.13b	v.21b	vv.30-31
But . . . *YHWH* with-holds judge-ment, protects *YHWH's* name	v.9	v.14	v.22	___

In Ezekiel's telling of Israel's history, the reoccurring action of *YHWH* suspending divine judgement— of the sequence (cf. v. 9, 14, and 22)—is absent in the final period of Israel's story.

Notable too is that at each stage and in each action sequence Ezekiel subverts the accepted national myth and twists it into a parody.

1. In the first period (vv. 5-9), instead of the received interpretation that Israel was elected before the

exodus from Egypt and committed apostasy with the golden calf after the exodus, Ezekiel insists that *in the moment of the exodus itself* both Israel and the Egyptians deserved judgement. Except for *YHWH's* concern for the divine reputation, Israel too would have perished in Egypt (cf. vv. 8b-9). "For Ezekiel, the Israelites walked out of Egypt under the suspended anger of the very God who was delivering them."[2]

2. In the second period (vv. 10–17), the same generation of the exodus receives two great gifts: the law, as the source of life (cf. vv.11, 13, 21) and the Sabbath, as the sign of the covenant and as the ethos of Israel's social and economic life (reflected in the ameliorating social-economic practices of the seventh day, the sabbatical year, and the Jubilee observations). Strikingly, here Ezekiel projects history backward; he decides that the oppression and exploitation under Israel's monarchy should be pushed back to the first exodus generation's rejection of *YHWH's* law and Sabbaths.

3. In the third period (vv. 18–26), the second generation in the wilderness proved no better than their parents. "But the children rebelled against me; they did not follow my statutes, and were not careful to observe my ordinances, by whose observance everyone shall live; they profaned my sabbaths" (Ezek 20:20, NRSV). In fact, Israel enters the land under the thoroughly unhappy scowl of a divine landlord who has judged them unfit inhabitants but suspended their sentence nevertheless. As one commentator states: "The prophet has telescoped eight or nine centuries of

2. Wright, *The Message of Ezekiel*, 158.

national history into one cryptic statement and retro-jected it on Israel's desert experience."[3]

4. In the fourth period (vv. 27–31), Israel's recent history is no better—its centuries of idolatry on high places are tantamount to fundamental and fatal disloyalty. "The exile, on this interpretation, was not some inexplicable surprise. It was simply Yahweh blowing the final whistle after a greatly extended period of injury time."[4] In v.30 and beyond Ezekiel leans in to address directly the elders sitting with him: the worst of the same historic sins are being practiced here and now.

When the history lesson is over, the prosecution's case is finished, and it ends with no word of *YHWH's* judgement being withheld.

Echoing Moses' pleading with God to think of his own name and reputation (cf. Ex 32:12), *YHWH* suspends judgement three times in Ezekiel's version of history, but no longer.

There is a momentary grace in Ezekiel's conclusion to the chapter, but it is a severe grace, in direct confrontation of Israel's idolatry. He declares that a new version of Israel's history will be told in the future. There will be a new exodus, but one that will be undertaken amidst great wrath and a new, purging wilderness experience (20:30–44). There is some sorting to be done, so that the remnant will finally know that *YHWH* is the Lord. The bigger point is this: God is not excusing Israel this time with the goal in mind of God's universal mission to include all the nations. Israel's future restoration will become a witness to the whole world (cf. Ezek 20:41).

3. Block, *The Book of Ezekiel*, 636.

4. Wright, *The Message of Ezekiel*, 160.

What do we do with Ezekiel 20? Along with Ezekiel 16, 23? Did this ecstatic priest-prophet get it right? As Wright wonders, did Ezekiel "go too far? Has he not engaged in distortion of the story? Who got it right, the great epic narratives, which at least include some glorious and positive periods alongside the more negative ones, or Ezekiel, with his unrelieved picture of rebellion, depravity and betrayal?"[5]

Perhaps Ezekiel perceives that he faces a dreadful task, and from the box of available tools he chooses those with the most oratorical punch. This exiled people had taken hold of a dangerous, triumphalist misinterpretation of their early and recent history. He was convinced that the scale of this complete misinterpretation of their history with *YHWH* could only be met by a shockingly direct confrontation, in which they finally and fiercely received their just desserts.

Ezekiel dares to tamper with the founding story of Israel. Matthew's Jesus performed a succinct version of the same with his parable of the tenants in the vineyard—he took the official story of Israel, changed its flavor, and tacked on a very different ending, immediately provoking his audience (Matt 21:33–46).

We are supposedly wiser these days, and the growing list of ecclesiastical apologies attests to at least several profoundly different tellings of Christian history. Like some of you, I grew up with the triumphant accounts of the faith, from the missions of the Celts, Nestorians, and Moravians, to the grand global expansion of the nineteenth and twentieth-century missionaries.

Perhaps we are now the elders sitting in Ezekiel's portico, as he drags before us the horrors and obscenities of

5. Wright, *The Message of Ezekiel*, 166.

religious wars, Crusades, pogroms, and Inquisitions, and confronts us with centuries of religious bigotry, burnings, drownings, cleansings, and cultural assimilation.

I wonder if Ezekiel may be more our foe here than friend. But perhaps he remains, precisely in that role, God's prophet to us. Are we being sorted now, too, as God's children? Are our founding myths being reinterpreted and reshaped to be more truthful?

May God's grace persist with us, in our failures, in our repentance, in our learning, and in our reconciliation with others.

Scripture: Ezekiel 20

Questions for Further Reflection:

1. Compare Ezekiel 20 to the exodus account in the Book of Exodus. What is similar? What is different? How might Ezekiel's revisions startle and provoke his original community? If well heard, how might they startle and provoke my own community?

2. What revisionary stories do we tell each other within our family, our church, or our larger community? What "grand failures" are missing from these "grand narratives?"

3. What prophetic revisions might be required of our own origin stories and worldviews—family, church, community, nation—to realign them with God's story about us in our present place and land?

10

How to (and How Not to) Pastor

Judy Paulsen

As has been noted earlier in this meditation series, Ezekiel was called to prophesy to Judean exiles living in Babylon toward the end of the sixth century BC. For close to two decades he challenged them to return to God, admit their sin, repent of their wickedness and start walking in God's ways.

In our text, Ezekiel 34, the prophet focusses in on a scathing assessment of Israel's shepherds, a common metaphor for leaders throughout Scripture. And while Ezekiel was critiquing both the royal and priestly leaders of Israel, as those called to serve in today's church, we too should pay particular attention to Ezekiel chapter 34.

As I sat down to write this meditation, the story gripping every major news outlet was the historic gathering at the Vatican addressing the sexual abuse of children, nuns, and seminarians by Roman Catholic bishops and priests. The sordid details of molestation, degradation, and rape were laid bare for the world to read and hear. For the better part of a week the TV cameras were focused on grown men and women weeping with the memory of things done to them decades ago.

But Catholics weren't the only ones making headlines. The Southern Baptists were also reported to be facing sexual assault charges brought against senior pastors and youth pastors by 700 victims from across the United States.[1]

The words of Ezekiel 34 ring out:

"Thus says the Lord God: Ah, you shepherds . . . who have been feeding yourselves! . . . You eat the fat, you clothe yourselves with the wool, you slaughter the fatlings; but you do not feed the sheep." (NRSV, vv. 2–4)

What were the pastors, priests and bishops thinking? How could this happen?

Well, it's an age-old story really. Leaders using their positions of authority and trust to satiate their sexual appetites.

But of course those are not the only appetites church leaders have satisfied.

There have been a string of news stories over the past decade exposing the appetites of megachurch pastors. Appetites for mansions, private jets, and huge salaries. Then, just this past month, an all-expenses-paid big game hunt was revealed to be on the menu for one celebrity pastor in Chicago.

"You . . . have been feeding yourselves!" cries out Ezekiel.

Closer to home, there is the travesty of church-run residential schools—many surrounded by the unmarked graves of Canada's indigenous children who died there. Some, we now know, died of starvation or beatings or lack of medical attention.

1. Zauzmer and Lati, "Southern Baptists' sexual abuse scandal."

The schools leave behind a legacy of generational trauma, stolen identity, lost language—to say nothing of all the rest that often went on there. Recently I had breakfast with a man who was escorted to one of these schools when he was just six years old.

"You have not strengthened the weak, you have not healed the sick, you have not bound up the injured." (v. 4)

Closer still, Ezekiel 34 has words of judgement for leaders of many *ordinary* churches dotting North America in our time.

Many of our churches have grown almost completely huddled. Many of the pastors and priests have become so focused on caring for the remaining flock and just trying to keep the doors open, that they long ago gave up any expectation that the church might reach out with the gospel, even to the people living within a block of their church buildings.

Close to 80 percent of the Canadian population now has no connection to a community of faith and little to no understanding of Christian teaching. The people ticking the "no religion" box on the last national census are the fastest growing sector in society today. Yet most Christians fail to share the faith with anyone, and most churches are failing to connect with the unchurched people around them.

Ezekiel's words ring out again,

"[Y]ou have not brought back the strayed, you have not sought the lost." (v. 4)

The lost! It's a term rarely spoken from our pulpits today. And yet there is so much evidence of "lostness" all around us.

It is into the muck and misery of all of this that we hear the terrifying word spoken in verse 10 of our reading.

"Thus says the Lord God, I am against the shepherds."
And further,

"I will demand my sheep at their hand, and put a stop to their feeding the sheep; no longer shall the shepherds feed themselves. I will rescue my sheep from their mouths, so that they may not be food for them."

But then, thank God, we read these beautiful, reassuring words:

"I will rescue them from all the places to which they have been scattered . . . I will bring them out from the peoples . . . I will feed them with good pasture . . . I will seek the lost . . . I will bring back the strayed . . . I will bind up the injured . . . I will strengthen the weak . . . I will feed them with justice" (34:12–16).

This too is an age-old story isn't it? God himself doing what we fail to do?

But one surely has to ask, "Is there no end to God having to make right what we've made wrong? And what about the terrible carnage done by the bad shepherds along the way?"

Especially as Christians, as the church which claims to follow the Good Shepherd himself—what went wrong? What keeps going wrong among some Christian leaders?

Ezekiel 34 certainly paints a stark picture of the spiritual and moral bankruptcy among some shepherds. But this chapter also highlights three points that, if remembered, will prevent a pastor or priest from going down that path.

Firstly, remember that we are the shepherds, *not the owners* of the sheep. But remember too that *there is* an owner. These sheep belong to the Lord God Almighty. The more aware we are of his power, his majesty, his holiness, the better we will remember our proper role.

Secondly, remember that God himself has *called us too*, entrusting us with this role of shepherding, caring, and nurturing his sheep. We are to guide, protect, feed, strengthen, and tend to them. This role is not a right but a privilege.

And most importantly, remember that our role as shepherds is to be subservient to and patterned after the very definition of good shepherding that God himself has shown to us.

Verse 23 says this:

"I will set up over them one shepherd, my servant David."

Ezekiel (living 400 years after David) was not predicting a resurrected King David. He was pointing to the coming Messiah, the Christ to whom Isaiah also referred when he wrote:

"He will feed his flock like a shepherd; he will gather the lambs in his arms, and carry them in his bosom, and gently lead the mother sheep." (Isaiah 40:11)

The One truly Good Shepherd—this is exactly who we see in Jesus and in his ministry as Matthew's gospel tells us:

"When he saw the crowds, he had compassion on them, because they were harassed and helpless, like sheep without a shepherd." (Matthew 9:36)

And this Messiah figure, promised in Ezekiel, is who Jesus plainly claimed to be when he said,

"I am the good shepherd. The good shepherd lays down his life for the sheep." (John 10:11)

What this means for us who are called to serve the church is this: the only way for us to shepherd as God would have us shepherd is to offer ourselves, body, mind, and soul to the Messiah, the Good Shepherd, who promises to come and live in us, guide, correct, strengthen, and heal us.

We need to give ourselves, every day, to Christ, and be formed in him. There is no other way for us to do this task.

I doubt that a single one of those Catholic priests or Baptist pastors set out at the start of their ministry to do such harm. But somewhere along the way they became disconnected from the One, the only One, who shepherds exactly as his heavenly Father desires.

Our Lord Jesus Christ is the One to be yoked to. He is the One to study. He is the One to love.

The closer we draw to him the more clearly we will see our own deficiencies. And there will be deficiencies.

None of us will get it completely right. You will undoubtedly make some significant mistakes yourself. But the more we give over to him, the better we will be as shepherds of his flock, who as motley as they are, are also the light of the world.

And at the end of time, John's Revelation says that the Good Shepherd will lead time itself to its full consummation and will make things fully right.

> "[F]or the Lamb at the center of the throne will
> be their shepherd, and he will guide them to
> springs of the water of life, and God will wipe
> away every tear from their eyes." (Rev. 7:17)

In agreement, Ezekiel so beautifully affirms that word,

"I will make with them a covenant of peace . . . I will make them . . . a blessing; and I will send down the showers in their season; they shall be showers of blessing . . . They shall know that I, the Lord their God, am with them" (Ezek 34:25–26, 30).

"You are my sheep, the sheep of my pasture and I am your God, says the Lord God." (v. 31)

Let us now shepherd according to the way of the Good Shepherd, for the sake of the world he loves.

Scripture: Ezekiel 34

Questions for Further Reflection:

1. Who has pastored you in the way of the Good Shepherd?

2. What specific things did they do to feed you, bind up your wounds, care for you, guide you, or protect you?

3. Who have you shepherded in the faith in similar fashion?

4. Pray for someone you know who has yet to come to faith. Ask God to show you some part you can play in them coming to know him.

11

God Has Only One Gig!

ANNETTE BROWNLEE

EZEKIEL 37 IS, PERHAPS, the best known chapter in the book of Ezekiel. Children have been singing a version of the African-American spiritual "Dem Dry Bones" since the Myers Jubilee Singers first recorded it in 1928. Christians in churches which celebrate an Easter Vigil service have been hearing this passage read in the context of Christ's resurrection since the fourth century.

Jerome declared that "all the churches of Christ" should read this passage.[1] It is easy to see why. It is certainly the climax of Ezekiel's prophecy, some say of all the Old Testament. As we stand with Ezekiel among these scattered bones and look backward to God's history with Israel and forward to God's history with Jesus and the church, the same singular conviction is apparent, which we must reckon with.

All of it, *all of it*, is God's action.

Maybe it takes a pile of dried bones resurrected into a people to make clear in our human centric world the primacy of God's initiative. While this story is for us it is not

1. Quoted in Stevenson and Glerup, *Ezekiel, Daniel*, 122.

about us; Ezekiel 37 is about God's actions, the ways God gives us to know him, and the reasons for the gift of divine recognition.

You know the story. Through the Spirit God leads Ezekiel out to a valley full of scattered dry bones. This might seem a more benign vision than many of those my colleagues had to contend with in this meditation series. But not so with a closer glance. Jeremiah had prophesied earlier, "The corpses of this people will be food for the birds of the air, and for the animals of the earth; and no one will frighten them away." (Jer 7:33, NRSV) These bones have been picked clean by carrion birds and scattered along the valley. No intact skeletons, no bits of remaining flesh or clothes for identification.

Israel is unrecognizable. Without the ability to know God. To repent. To hope. To create a future.

But God is not done with them. How can God give them up, even in the death of their disobedience?

"Can these bones live?" God asks the Spirit-led Ezekiel. And Ezekiel rightly answers, "You alone know." (Ezek 37:3, NIV)

And live they do! Ambrose says quite simply, "God has the power to raise up the dead."[2] But the character of that new life is what we must listen for, if this is to be God's word to us in our day.

2. Ambrose, *On the Holy Spirit*, 3.19. "God has the power to raise up the dead. For, 'as the Father raiseth up the dead, and giveth life; so the Son also giveth life to whom he will.' Moreover, the Spirit also raises up, through whom God raises up, for it is written: 'He shall quicken also your mortal bodies, because of his Spirit dwelling in you.' Yet, that you may not think this a weak grace, hear that the Spirit also raises up, for the Prophet Ezechiel says: 'Come, spirit, and blow upon these dead, and they will live. And I prophesied as he had commanded me; and the spirit of life came into them, and they lived, and they stood up upon their feet, an exceeding great assembly.'"

We hear four characteristics—or stages—of this resurrection. In four stages in chapter 37, God breathes life into this pile of dry bones through the word of his prophet.

First, Ezekiel preaches to the bones, and from the dust God connects the knee bone to the thigh bone and the bones come back together (vv. 7–8).

Second, Ezekiel preaches to the four winds; then God puts breath into the reconnected bones, and the scattered bones now stand as a multitude (vv. 9–10).

It is at this point that God identifies these bones. "Mortal, these bones are the whole house of Israel." (v. 11, NRSV) Only now do they speak, and what they say surprises us. We might expect repentance or thanksgiving. Instead what we hear in this verse is a cry of lament. "Our bones are dried up, and our hope is lost; we are cut off completely."

In the third stage, God hears their cries and promises hope and a future. "Thus says the Lord God: I am going to open your graves, and bring you up from your graves, O my people; and I will bring you back to the land of Israel. . . . I will place you on your own soil." (vv. 12–14)

The fourth stage is described in the oracle which follows this passage. It is the last sign-act in the book. At God's command Ezekiel takes two sticks, one for the southern kingdom and another for the northern kingdom, and then God declares that when he brings the exiles back to their land he will make the two sticks one. (vv. 15–22) Never again shall they be divided. David will be set over them as their shepherd and God will make with them an everlasting covenant. God will dwell with them and be their God, and they will be his people. (vv. 24–28)

If this all sounds very familiar, it should. The resurrection of the dry bones is a recapitulation of God's history with creation and Israel, leading to a new creation and a new exodus that are both similar to and different from what came before. Not creation out of nothing but creation out of the nothingness of a dead people, who have died because of their own disobedience. Not an exodus from slavery in Egypt, but an exodus from slavery to sin and to the incapacity to listen to God.

It is the prerogative of God to raise the dead. And each of the four stages of resurrection here: bones (vv. 7–8), breath (vv. 9–10), deliverance (vv. 12–14), and reconciliation under a new covenant (vv. 15–28), is God's act. Divine initiative and nothing else. Why? Ezekiel states clearly and repeatedly the reason for God's actions, even three times in our passage. God tells Ezekiel that when he does these things, then his people "shall know that I am the Lord . . . then you shall know that I, the Lord, have spoken and will act" (vv. 13–14, cf. v. 6). And I could go on with more and more examples, for this phrase about divine recognition occurs more times in Ezekiel than any other book of the Old Testament.[3] Divine initiative, whether bringing judgement to death or mercy to new life, is given for the purpose of divine recognition. "Then you shall *know* that I, the Lord, have spoken and will act."

What are we to make of all this, as a word for us in our day? This four-fold character of resurrected life? This divine initiative leading to our recognition of God? Let me offer three points.

First, this story calls us to an enormous degree of humility about *our* capacity to know God. It is good to hear this in our various church settings. This story makes it clear that none of the preconditions for recognition of God reside in human beings or in human understanding. They

3. Zimmerli, "Knowledge of God," 30-31.

lie totally within divine initiative. All the ways we think *we* can know God through our intuition, our experience, our dreams or doctrine—name your favorite—are thrown on their heads. Bones cannot hear, cannot intuit, cannot argue, cannot pray. Bones cannot go to an alpha group, sing praise songs or Anglican chant, or read old texts or original languages. They cannot analyze the culture or reflect on mission strategies, cannot explore the psychological need for God, or human restlessness. You get the point.

The resurrection of the dry bones is not only a statement of God's marvelous response to Israel's disobedience. It is a statement against Israel's capacity—and our capacity—to know God through our own initiative and efforts. Those dead bones can hear Ezekiel's prophetic word *only because God has made it so through the Holy Spirit.* We too must pray, "Come, Holy Spirit come." If the mantra of our post-modern age is, "I think, therefore I am," this story cuts that off at its knees and offers us a different mantra, "God acts and therefore we live."

God is and remains Lord of our knowledge and recognition of him.

Second, the new life God gives us in Jesus Christ, through our union with him, is somehow contained and prefigured in the history of God's actions with creation and Israel. Our life in Jesus Christ is not some other life, free-floating and untethered to the story of creation and God's history with Israel. No, God has only one gig, it seems, and this is it.

At first it might seem hard to know how this applies in the context of our passage, Ezekiel 37. But if we turn to Ephesians 2, where Paul describes the new life we have in Jesus, it all begins to sound familiar. Some even think Paul had Ezekiel 37 in mind when he composed Ephesians chapter 2. Paul tells us that we were "dead" in our trespasses and sin (2:1). We were—echoing the lament of the resurrected bones of Israel—without hope (cf. Ezek 37:11). Then in his mercy God made us alive in Jesus Christ (Eph 2:5). And the character of that life? Well, Ezekiel has described it for us already. It is most clearly discerned in a resurrected body. In raising Jesus from the dead, God connects the knee bone of his Son's body to the hip bone. And we too, Paul tells us, have a foretaste of this since God has "made us alive together with Christ" and "raised us up with him." (Eph 2:5–6)

And this redemptive pattern from Ezekiel continues even further. This raised-up people of God, the church, becomes the place where the "two sticks" of Jew and Gentile become one new humanity in Jesus Christ (3:6; cf. Ezek 37:15–17). And the reason for this marvelous divine initiative? We know that too. So that in the ages to come we might *know* the immeasurable riches of his grace in kindness toward us in Christ Jesus (cf. Eph 2:7). As we evangelize and disciple, and as we are drawn deeper into Christ's life, that life has a shape and pattern, the very same shape and pattern we see in Ezekiel.

Finally, we know God through God's actions. This is the only kind of knowledge of which Ezekiel speaks. Even with the strange and at times mystical visions of this prophet—spinning wheels within wheels, eating food cooked over dung, dancing bones—God reveals himself through actions embedded in the life of Israel and the church throughout history. *God's actions, through his Word, are his self-introduction.* "I will put my spirit within you, and you shall live, and I will place you on your own soil; then you shall know that I, the Lord, have spoken and will act, says the Lord." (Ezek 37:14) Looking forward to Easter, we will hear again the story on which all of our hopes are placed. Death, even the death of our disobedience does not—and will never—have the last word in our lives or in the world. The dead bones of Jesus live. And so do ours. The Psalm many churches will sing on Easter is Psalm 118:24. Ezekiel would be pleased: "On this day the Lord has acted, we will rejoice and be glad in it."

Rejoice? Yes. Be glad? Yes. Pass it on? We're trying our best. It is God's prerogative to raise the dead and in this is our hope. Ezekiel reminds us that God acts so we can recognize him. So we can say in our day with the centurion at the foot of the cross, who saw with his own eyes the prerogative of God in full bloom, "Truly this man is the son of God" (Mark 15:39).

Scripture: Ezekiel 37

Questions for Further Reflection

1. Think of some times that you have experience renewal in your own life? Can you see God as the ultimate source of that renewal?

2. Have we realized our incapacity to know God apart from God's own initiative? How would a deeper awareness of this reality affect our prayer life and the life of our churches?

3. The Christian conviction discussed here is that "God has only one gig." That is, a singular goal and pattern is discernable in God's work of redemption throughout history. Can reflecting on the pattern of resurrection-life, discerned in both Ezekiel 37 and Ephesians 2, help us grow deeper in our own awareness of God's active presence?

12

Beyond All Measure

Thomas Power

Shortly after taking power in France in 1799, Napoleon Bonaparte told his Minister of the Interior, Jean-Antoine Chaptal: "I want to do something great and useful for Paris." Chaptal replied, "Give it water." Napoleon seemed surprised, but he went on to guarantee free water, requiring fountains to run unrestrictedly, night and day, and all restaurants to provide free water to customers.[1]

Similarly in Ezekiel 47, I believe that God does something great, new, and useful and that this has a lot to do with water and what water represents.

In the first half of the book of Ezekiel, in a series of extraordinary visions, we are given a message declaring the glory of God's sovereign rule, but also the promise of judgment, the fall of Jerusalem, and the withdrawal of that same glory. In the last section of the book, all of this gives way to hope. Despair gives way to restoration.

Specifically, chapters 40 to 48 are the climax of the whole book; their focus is a vision of the new temple where God returns in glory to be in the midst of his people. This

1. "Paris under Napoleon."

new temple is carefully measured; it is perfect, and without flaw (cf. Ezek 40–42). It has much the same layout and function as the previous temple with its worship, offerings, sacrifices, priestly caste, and feasts reinstated.

Yet suddenly, here in Ezekiel 47, we are given something strange and new. Water emerges from the place of God's altar, begins as a trickle, goes beneath the door of the temple, and soon increases in volume, transforming the dry ground and bringing abundance, growth, and healing.

This is all very different from what has gone before.

What is this river? What does it all mean?

Three features stand out:

Increase (vv. 1-6)

First, the volume of water increases as it flows.

The initial source of water is a trickle from under the altar of the temple. The flow begins gently but gathers force once *outside* the sanctuary. Then it increases in depth as it proceeds: from ankle, to knee, to waist. Finally, its depth is so great that it overwhelms Ezekiel. A trickle is transformed into a torrent.

In four separate stages, the figure accompanying Ezekiel in this vision measures a distance of one thousand cubits from the temple precincts (that is, four segments equivalent to about 457 meters or 1500 feet each). Ezekiel enters the water and as his distance from the temple increases (one thousand cubits, two thousand cubits, and so so) he reports the water's depth. The water deepens the further out he wades, increasing from "knee-deep," then up to his waist, until the water becomes "deep enough to swim in." (v. 5, NRSV)

In reading this, one should keep in mind that the number 4 is one of wholeness and totality throughout Ezekiel. For example, one encounters four living creatures with four faces (1:5–6); four wheels that travel in the four directions of the compass (1:15–17). But here any standard of completeness is exceeded. With this deluge of water, what at first could be measured becomes immeasurable. As Ezekiel wades out further and further, the depth of the water becomes too deep to measure. It becomes, we are told, "a river that I could not cross." (v.5) No human standard of measure can be used to fathom the overwhelming amount of water. It is beyond human capacity to contain or control. It is beyond measure.

Abundance (vv. 7-11)

The second feature has to do with growth and abundance.

What is the purpose of all this increased volume of water?

In this desert land, the water flow produces trees on each side (v. 7). They bear fruit not just once or twice a year, but every month (v. 12). Growth is continuous.

The water is fresh and life-giving, enlivening even the waters of the lifeless Dead Sea. Remember the waters of the Dead Sea lie hundreds of meters below sea level. Fish can't live there because of the large amounts of salt. It is a lifeless place afflicted with, seemingly, a curse of God, a place of judgment. But now it is transformed into a life-giving lake with an abundance of fish. It will be as rich in its number of fish as the great sea, the Mediterranean. Further, there will be a variety of fish species: "Wherever the river goes, every living creature . . . will live" (v. 9), we are told.

More surprising still, even a residue of salt supply, useful as a preservative, will be kept: "[I]ts swamps and marshes will not become fresh; they are to be left for salt" (v. 11), we are told.

The course of the water has a miraculous effect. In every place where the river reaches there is life (v. 9). What was dead is made alive.

Healing (v. 12)

Thirdly, not only does the increase in volume bring abundance, but it also brings healing. Such life-giving waters bring about life-giving trees on either bank of the flowing river. And the purpose of these trees, bearing fruit continuously, whose leaves never wither, is to bring healing. Now, not only the fish, but all creatures that gather wherever the healing waters reach will have life (v. 12).

ॐ

So out of God's temple flows a great life-giving river bordered by trees whose fruit is for food and whose leaves are for healing. Here we have blessings linked with the divine presence, expressed in the fertility of fruit trees and fresh water, leaves for healing, fish for fishermen, and life-preserving salt. What we are given here is a vision of life-giving abundance. Healing. Preservation. Prosperity. Life beyond measure.

Beyond the Temple

To understand the significance of all this, we have to consider the context of Ezekiel 40–46. These chapters are preoccupied with the precise measurement and building plans for the restored temple, along with a detailed accounting of its rituals.

But here in Ezekiel 47, precision and detail is surpassed by a vision of a God who shows that his life-giving presence extends outside the confines of his own sanctuary. Traditionally the altar in the temple was the place to present something to God. Here God reverses that practice. The water flow begins in the temple but does not remain there; rather it flows away from God in a generous act of giving. The message is that renewal of life goes out from the place of the divine presence into the surrounding land.

This is all a surprise since up to now there has been a concentration on the sanctuary as a place where holiness is guarded carefully with the ritual and sacrificial system. But here we are shown that God's reach goes beyond the temple. God's presence in his sanctuary located in the midst of his people does *not* create a self-contained holy place. Rather God proceeds beyond the confines of the temple to bring abundance, life, and healing of the land.

God's Grace beyond Measure

What extends from the temple cannot be contained within measurable confines, but bursts forth in exceeding and overwhelming amounts, all emblematic of a mighty power emanating from God.

If earlier God's anger was comprehensive and complete (as Prof. Radner shows in his meditation on Ezekiel 5), shocking in its force and in its inclusiveness of good and bad, then here in chapter 47 that anger is reversed. For here we find that the torrent of God's judgment—previously visceral against Israel—has become a torrent of blessing redirected to Israel's benefit.

The image is one of growth beyond measure. God lets loose life, healing, and fruitfulness far beyond the temple boundaries into the wider world. The vision is of a river of grace, overflowing and limitless. As it flows it becomes uncontainable and in its flow individuals, societies, and creation are caught up and revived. The renewal and hope taking place is infinite, beyond measure. In all this, God acts and exceeds our expectations.

In a profound way it signals to us that God's power and grace are open to all with no walls, no barriers, in a free-flowing, increasing, and generous outpouring of love in the renewal of creation. Grace is not containable but overflows and covers all.

John, in his apocalyptic vision, also sees the river of the water of life, fruit trees that continually bear fruit, and leaves for the healing of the nations (Rev 22:1–2). But John has a vision of an even greater hope: a completely new creation. Like Ezekiel's vision of the restored Jerusalem, in John's depiction of the heavenly city, the New Jerusalem, abundance and healing are found. But unlike Ezekiel, the New Jerusalem in Revelation is without a temple for it has disappeared (Rev 21:1–8). Instead God and the Lamb will be the temple of the community, and abundance and healing will be found in every place that God dwells with his people. Now the river of life flows outward, not from the temple, but from the very throne of God and of the Lamb right down the main street of the city.

Jesus

As a foretaste of John's vision Jesus declares himself to be the source of living water to all who believe (John 7:37–39), saying further: "I have come that they may have life and have it *abundantly*" (John 10:10). But it is not only that they should receive new life, but that this new life, like the water from the temple, should flow from within them. Jesus teaches us, "Whoever believes in me, as the Scripture says, 'Out of his heart will flow rivers of living water.'" (John 7:38, ESV)

Here we have a picture of the kind of impact God wants believers to have. God blesses not simply to make us feel good, but to carry his blessing further. Adapting Napoleon's declaration, God is in essence saying to you and to me: "I want to do something great and useful for the world through you." He is inviting us to become channels of blessing. Like the river, Jesus gives blessing and life on receipt of which believers in turn are meant to be a blessing to the world. We receive, and then we pass on the blessing. And that blessing should see an increase, bringing further abundance and healing. Such renewal and restored hope is potentially infinite, beyond measure.

It is important to realize the infinite nature of God's blessing outlined here. Are we ready to receive that blessing, knowing that on receipt of it we should act so that it does not merely stay with us? Are we prepared to act on what that blessing demands?

Scripture: Ezekiel 47

Questions for Further Reflection:

1. Ezekiel's river evokes the river of paradise which watered the Garden of Eden (cf. Gen 2:8–14). In what sense does Ezekiel 47:1–12 involve a restoration of that first garden?

2. Running water is called "living" in Hebrew. In the New Testament this image becomes "water of life."

Read the following passages: John 4:7–15; John 7:37–38; Rev 21:6; and Rev 22:17. How do these passages guide your understanding of water and what water signifies in the Bible?

3. The early Fathers of the church viewed the river flowing from the temple as representing different things. For one, it represented the increase in the number of believers; for another, the four-fold measuring sequence pointed to the four gospels, the depth of the last measurement being the depth of John's gospel; for another still, the river stood for baptism; and finally, for another the river was an image of the teaching of the church and of the grace of baptism. In light of the meditation above, do any of these views have merit?

4. What answer would you give to the request: "I want to do something great and useful for the world through you"?

Bibliography

Ambrose. *The Holy Spirit*. Translated by Roy J. Deferrari. In *Saint Ambrose: Theological and Dogmatic Works*, 31–214. The Fathers of the Church 44. Washington D.C.: Catholic University of America Press, 1963.

Block, Daniel I. *The Book of Ezekiel: Chapters 1-24*. The New International Commentary of the Old Testament. Grand Rapids: Eerdmans, 1997.

Broome, Edwin C. "Ezekiel's Abnormal Personality." *Journal of Biblical Literature* 65 (1946) 277–292.

Brueggemann, Walter. *The Prophetic Imagination*. 2d ed. Minneapolis: Fortress, 2001.

Carson, D. A., et al. *New Bible Commentary*. Downers Grove, IL: InterVarsity, 1994.

Clements, Ronald E. *Ezekiel*. Westminster Bible Companion. Louisville: Westminster John Knox, 1996.

Green, Michael P., ed. *Illustrations for Biblical Preaching*. Grand Rapids: Baker, 1989.

Gunnars, Kris. "Why Ezekiel Bread Is the Healthiest Bread You Can Eat." https://www.healthline.com/nutrition/ezekiel-bread

Halperin, David J. *Seeking Ezekiel: Text and Psychology*. University Park, PA: Penn State University Press, 1993.

Jenson, Robert W. *Ezekiel*. Brazos Theological Commentary on the Bible. Grand Rapids: Brazos Press, 2009.

Jerome, *Letter 108*.

Kaiser, Walter C. Jr., and Duane Garrett, eds. *Archaeological Study Bible: An Illustrated Walk through Biblical History and Culture*. Grand Rapids: Zondervan, 2005.

Lapsley, Jacqueline E. "Ezekiel." In *Women's Bible Commentary*, edited by Carol A. Newsom, Sharon H. Ringe, and Jacqueline E. Lapsley, 283–292. Louisville: Westminster John Knox, 2012.

Lewis, C.S. *Perelandra*. New York: Scribner Classics, 1996.

Origen. *Homily on Ezekiel 1*. Translated by Mischa Hooker. In *Exegetical Works on Ezekiel*, Edited by Roger Pearse, 8–67. Ipswich, UK: Cheiftain Publishing, 2014. https://www.roger-pearse.com/weblog/wp-content/uploads/2018/07/Origen-Homilies_on_Ezekiel-ed_Hooker-2014.pdf

Stetzer, Ed. "Avoiding the Pitfall of Syncretism." The Exchange with Ed Stetzer. https://www.christianitytoday.com/edstetzer/2014/june/avoiding-pitfall-of-syncretism.html

Stevenson, Kenneth and Michael Glerup, eds. *Ezekiel, Daniel*. Ancient Christian Commentary on Scripture: Old Testament 13. Downers Grove, IL: InterVarsity, 2008.

Stiebert, Johanna. *The Exile and the Prophet's Wife: Historic Events and Marginal Perspectives*. Interfaces. Collegeville, MN: Liturgical Press, 2005.

Taylor, Charles. *A Secular Age*. Cambridge, MA: Belknap, 2007.

Taylor, J. Glen. "Was Yahweh Worshiped as the Sun?" *Biblical Archaeology Review* 20 (1994) 52–61, 90–91.

———. *Yahweh and the Sun: Biblical and Archaeological Evidence for Sun Worship in Ancient Israel*. Journal for the Study of the Old Testament: Supplement Series 111. Sheffield: Sheffield Academic Press, 1993.

Taylor, Marion Ann. "Ezekiel." In *The IVP Women's Bible Commentary*, edited by Catherine Clark Kroeger and Mary J. Evans, 396–421. Downers Grove, IL: InterVarsity, 2002.

Walton, John H. and Craig S. Keener, eds. *The NIV Cultural Backgrounds Study Bible*. Grand Rapids: Zondervan, 2016.

Wright, Christopher J. H. *The Message of Ezekiel: A New Heart and a New Spirit*. The Bible Speaks Today. Downers Grove, IL: IVP Academic, 2001.

Zauzmer, Julie and Marisa Iati. "Southern Baptists' sexual abuse scandal prompts calls for criminal investigations, comparisons to Catholics." https://www.washingtonpost.com/religion/2019/02/12/southern-baptists-sexual-abuse-scandal-prompts-calls-criminal-investigations-comparisons-catholics/?utm_term=.cob455b4f481

Zimmerli, Walther. "Knowledge of God according to the Book of Ezekiel." Translated by Douglas W. Stott. In *I am Yahweh*, 29–98. Eugene, OR: Wipf&Stock, 2018.

Zoba, Wendy Murray. "Separate and Equal." *Christianity Today* 40 (1996) 14–24.

"Paris under Napoleon." Wikipedia, last modified February 27 2019. https://en.wikipedia.org/wiki/Paris_under_Napoleon